Legislative Foundations
of American
Consumer Society

Legislative Foundations of American Consumer Society

Regulation, Deregulation and Their Impacts from the 1930s to Today

BOB SULLIVAN

McFarland & Company, Inc., Publishers
Jefferson, North Carolina

ISBN (print) 978-1-4766-8588-5
ISBN (ebook) 978-1-4766-4405-9

LIBRARY OF CONGRESS AND BRITISH LIBRARY
CATALOGUING DATA ARE AVAILABLE

Library of Congress Control Number 2021043204

© 2021 Bob Sullivan. All rights reserved

No part of this book may be reproduced or transmitted in any form or by any means, electronic or mechanical, including photocopying or recording, or by any information storage and retrieval system, without permission in writing from the publisher.

Front cover: Senate Banking and Currency Committee hearing on May 26, 1933 (Everett Collection); aerial view of suburban sprawl in Las Vegas, Nevada (Iofoto/Shutterstock)

Printed in the United States of America

*McFarland & Company, Inc., Publishers
Box 611, Jefferson, North Carolina 28640
www.mcfarlandpub.com*

For my wife Karin

Table of Contents

Preface 1
Introduction 3

Part One—The Regulatory Society

1. Democrats and Republicans Before 1932 11
2. Glass-Steagall as Foundational Legislation 18
3. Joe T. Robinson's Home Owners' Loan Act 29
4. The 1934 Housing Act and "Redlining" 37
5. Wagner-Steagall and Public Housing 52
6. Steagall-Wagner and the Creation of "Fannie Mae" 60
7. The 1945 Amended GI Bill and American Racism 67
8. African American Exodus and the 1949 Housing Act 76
9. Explosion! Levittowns and Shopping Malls 88

Part Two—The Deregulated Society

10. The White Working Class and the "Treaty of Detroit" 99
11. Brown, Civil Rights and the End of the New Deal 109
12. The 1970s: New Republicans and Old Democrats 117
13. Depository Institutions and the Flowering of Bain Capital 125
14. The Privatized Mortgage Industry of the 2000s 135

Table of Contents

15. From Brooksley Born to Sarbanes-Oxley	143
16. Dodd-Frank and Legislative Approval of Consumer Society	152
Conclusions: The Consumer Paradise	161
Chapter Notes	165
Bibliography	173
Index	183

Preface

This book explores the legislative origins of modern American society as organized around the activity of consumption. What may not be self-evident is that the focus here is not on productivity, which prior to the mid–20th century was the mainstay of economics. This distinction is important because, since that time, Americans have been increasingly oriented toward consuming what other nations—especially China—produce. This tilting of the economic scales towards consumerism would not be possible if other nations (again, China) were not so dangerously unbalanced in the direction of "productionism." The two major powers in the global economy are thus MAD—case studies in Mutually Assured Destruction.

My original interest was limited to seven American laws passed between 1933 and 1949, with the focus on the legislative process, as a study in modern political science. By examining American consumer society in the context of seven key pieces of legislation, I was able to eliminate most discussion of intention. This had the effect of making modern American consumer society seem something of an afterthought or accident, as if our parents and grandparents all just woke up one morning in 1950 to discover a whole new world around them.

Taking a broader view, this book traces the growth of that world and the cultural learning process by which Americans removed their consumerist training-wheels and learned to pedal the shiny-new bicycle unassisted. I am still amazed to reflect that my grandmother did not know what a mortgage was while my granddaughter of eight years old has at least a sketchy idea of what the grown-ups are discussing when they talk about that kind of financing. Culture has indeed changed the ways in which our brains are wired.

Regarding my approach to researching this book, I would describe myself more an armchair philosopher than an archival digger. In due

Preface

deference to those of the latter category, I would add that if this book contributes to establishing the significance of an obscure economist named Winfield Riefler, I will be delighted. I probably would not have discovered Riefler had not John Maynard Keynes discovered him for me, and so discovering Keynes's brief note in Riefler's papers was one of those *eureka!* moments that makes the drudgery of archival digging a delight.

There are many fine books on American consumerism, so many that I prefer not to name any for fear of omitting some. I would, however, assert that this book is different by dint of its concentration on legislation and the legislative process. No other book that I know of sees modern American consumer society as the product of a gathering mass of legislative enactments resulting in something like Levittown, New York. In this book, the cookie-cutter suburban home is the focal point of American consumerism—without it such consumerism would not exist. I am happy to cede a kind of equality to the automobile, but I would not cede primacy of place to it. I pay adequate attention to Walter Reuther and the UAW, but not at the price of neglecting Bill Levitt.

I would like to acknowledge the many people who have helped this book along. For useful comments, I thank Sari Carel, Edwin Aquilar, Samantha Lewis, Susan Kalish, my friend Harold Sullivan, Elizabeth Cohen of Harvard University, Gabriel Dotto of Michigan State University, and Herbert Richardson of the Edwin Mellen Press.

I owe a measure of thanks to my two sons, Paul and Justin, who read and criticized earlier versions of this manuscript. If I needed a demonstration of their intellect and insight (I did not), they certainly provided it.

My wife Karin has given me direct criticism of ideas and their expression, but she has been at her best when talking about our grandchildren and slipping in an aside that functioned as a direct hit. She gave me more than she knows, and I thank her for that.

Introduction

This book should be and is described by its subtitle. It is about the regulation and deregulation of American consumer society. But however adequate, such a description begs the question: what is meant by the term *consumer society*, and so it should be answered before any more specific matters of regulation and deregulation are brought up.

My answer to that question refers the reader back to the late 19th century, when the theory of economics experienced a revolution of seismic proportions. Until about 1870, economics was a half-theory, one in which only the function of supply (or production) was measurable. The other half of the theory, comprising demand was still something of a mystery. Consumption was much talked about but nowhere near close to being measured.

Then overnight, as it were, several thinkers arrived at a technique called *marginal analysis* by which they were able to measure demand. In the 1890s, Alfred Marshall put supply and demand together on the same page in the form of a scissors diagram, argued that their relation could be depicted, and so he produced the first scientific economics textbook. By the term *science* I mean only that all major functions of the field could be measured.

In those decades at the latter part of the 19th century, at least the idea of a measurable consumer society was invented. All that remained was to actually create a functioning version of the model. The "Roaring Twenties" may have looked like a consumer society, but the consumption of that decade was indeed more roaring than measured, and so it did not conform to the model of economics produced in Alfred Marshall's 1890s textbook. It would first have to submit to regulation and with regulation, measurement. That change only occurred with the Great Depression of the 1930s.

The reader may disagree when I claim that the New Deal produced

Introduction

the world's first consumer society, but all I mean by that claim is a society that is regulated and is therefore measurable. I am quite aware that people of past centuries were avid consumers of outlandish clothing, entertainment by the likes of Mozart, second homes in the town of Bath, and gambling casinos in Baden-Baden, but such phenomena were not measured or if they were, the measurement lacked a coherent conceptual context. It was only in the New Deal that the Roosevelt administration produced a measurable (if not yet actually measured) consumer society.

The actual production of a consumer society then took seventeen years and ranged over seven pieces of federal legislation. The first was the 1933 Banking Act, better known as Glass-Steagall, which boxed investment banks out of certain markets like housing and gave the government the control it needed to measure the activities of the nation's savings & loan banks. The United States treaded water for six months with the passage of the Home Owners' Loan Act, but by 1934 it was ready for the nation's first Housing Act. That act led to nothing immediately but was popular and so set the table for more legislation. The fourth of the seven laws I mentioned earlier was the 1937 Housing Act, better known as Wagner-Steagall, which provided the basis of housing for persons not able to afford a mortgaged home. It was followed by the little known 1938 Housing Act, mischievously named Steagall-Wagner, which provided a means for fueling the 1934 Housing Act in the form of a federal agency nicknamed "Fannie Mae."

Matters became delayed when the war took center-stage, but aside from the casualties and destruction, it was in its legislative outcome just what the consumer society needed to get kick-started. By means of the GI Bill, fifteen million American veterans were eligible for no-down-payment home mortgages and so could buy a home and be more or less automatically qualified for the credit needed to purchase all the stuff that would furnish it. Homes suited to this kind of clientele still needed to be produced, and that detail was taken care of by builders like Bill Levitt, whose Levittown assembly line produced nearly 17,500 homes in four years.

In a racist society, there was still the not-small matter of where to allow African Americans, a detail that was addressed in the seventh and final law of the New Deal/Fair Deal period: the 1949 Housing Act. It authorized the building of 830,000 apartment units over the course of several years, but in something of a confusion of purpose that often occurs in legislation, the 1949 Housing Act also addressed

Introduction

slum-clearance and so authorized the demolition of nearly as many apartments as it built.

Also, it might be helpful to the reader to bunch and simplify these seven key laws, which I do here in the text rather than in footnote:

- 1933: Glass-Steagall (1933 Banking Act; the foundational legislation);
- 1933: Home Owners Loan Act (first to acknowledge home as American "Dream");
- 1934: Housing Act (enacts most federal guarantees for new home purchases);
- 1937: Wagner-Steagall (enacts first modern public housing authorization)
- 1938: Steagall-Wagner (authorizes fund-raising mechanism in "Fannie Mae");
- 1944: GI Bill (authorizes no down payment mortgages for White World War II veterans);
- 1949: Housing Act (authorizes slum-removal and new public housing units).

❖❖❖

By the 1950s, the United States had fully realized the world's first consumer society, dating these things from the marginalist revolution of the late 19th century. But then African Americans got "uppity" and challenged the entire arrangement, producing a second civil rights revolution that actually began in the same week the first civil rights movement ended with the assassination of Martin Luther King, Jr. The Fair Housing Act of 1968 was followed by several other pieces of legislation related to real estate loans, culminating in the 1977 Community Reinvestment Act. The chief value of this legislation for this book was that it demonstrated that the New Deal regulatory state could be dismantled, as important a lesson as has ever been dished out by Congress.

The neo liberal era of housing deregulation began in 1980 and continued for the next twenty years, culminating in the repeal of Glass-Steagall in 1999. With one exception, every program and principle of the New Deal/Fair Deal era was demolished. The one exception was consumer society itself. Neo-capitalism, the alternative term for neo-liberalism, prized the deregulated consumer society. No one lamented the demolition of those mom & pop affairs hailed in the 1946 Frank Capra film, *It's a Wonderful Life*, and just about everyone

Introduction

(it seemed) jumped on board the train headed for the 2008 wreck tellingly called the *Subprime Mortgage Crisis*. The Democrats passed legislation to deregulate the consumer economy, but since Dodd-Frank (also known as the Dodd-Frank Wall Street Reform and Consumer Protection Act) had few teeth, no one paid much attention. The deregulated consumer society, now free of its training wheels, continued to roll on. With the one exception of *Walmart*, it eventually freed itself of retail outlets and settled for daily deliveries of goods "made-in-China" by trucks marked Amazon Prime, Fed Ex, UPS, or the like. The full-blown economic picture would couple Chinese production with American consumption, but from the worms-eye view allowed to most of us, it all looks like a consumer society gone mad.

As was done before, it might help the reader to bunch the legislation of neo liberal society into a single picture. For the sake of symmetry, I again do this in seven pieces of legislation, omitting the Financial Institutions Reform, Recovery, and Enforcement Act, better known by its acronym of FIRREA. Again, for the reader's convenience, I list these pieces of legislation here in the text once again:

- 1968: Fair Housing Act (basic legislation for deregulating racism in home loans);
- 1977: Community Reinvestment Act (practical measures to end racism in home loans);
- 1980: DIDMCA (first dismantling of federal home loan guarantees);
- 1982: Garn-St. Germain (authorizes adjustable-rate home loans, or ARMs);
- 1999: Gramm-Leach-Bliley: (repeals Glass-Steagall);
- 2000: Commodity Futures Modernization Act (authorizes trade in derivatives);
- 2010: Dodd-Frank (promises reform of Wall Street and consumer protection).

◈ ◈ ◈

That's what this book is about, mainly. I also feel obliged to provide some explanation, and so I spend at least two chapters trying to deal with the two great American political parties. I am also intrigued by Werner Sombart's problem of why it is that the United States has no worker's party, since work is what most of us spend most of our time doing. The detours may be distracting to the book's main argument, but

Introduction

I think they enrich it, and so I have not buried those considerations in endnotes.

Here I would highlight the main message of these detours. Modern American consumer society would not have been possible without a revolution in the organization of American work. From skilled workers producing things to which they added their signatures, we mutated to lines of unskilled laborers assembling things with someone else's name on them or with a personal title like *Ford*. These unskilled laborers scattered along a dismembered supply-chain were the nation's first consumers. They reached the peak of their performance with the signing of the 1950 "Treaty of Detroit," which cemented a deal that had been developing since Henry Ford created the assembly line in 1913. Walter Reuther rose to prominence along with his CIO workers, and if I'm to guess right, he knew better than to negotiate the terms of the Treaty of Detroit with General Motors. Nonetheless, he still allowed it all to happen.

The reader would be right to notice that my concern for workers is reducible to a concern for the other half of the economic puzzle, namely, production. In this respect, workers have lost doubly. On the one hand, they have ceased being the creators dreamed of by William Morris and the other thinkers of the Arts and Crafts movement, and have been remade into the assemblers of CIO organized industrial unions. On the other hand, they have been remade into the consumers of other people's products, those other people often located in China's Guangdong province. What would Karl Marx have thought of the slogan: "Consumers of all lands unite! You have a world to win and nothing to lose!" We shall never know.

Part One

The Regulatory Society

1

Democrats and Republicans Before 1932

Entering the year 1932, the Democratic Party was still a southern and agrarian party, despite having nominated New York Governor Al Smith as their presidential candidate as recently as 1928. The party had elected few of the nation's presidents between the Civil War and the Great Depression, and when we remind ourselves that Woodrow Wilson was a Democrat, we also do well to recall that he ran as a northern governor and that he was helped to victory because the Republicans split and ran two candidates in the 1912 election. Wilson was no exception. With his racism, he very nearly proved the rule.

If we take the *southern* label first, that means not only that the party was strong in the South but also that the party was deeply entangled with the creation and defense of Dixie's culture. The latter featured not just as an unwillingness to face the loss of the Civil War but also a lively sense that defeat on the battlefield did not translate into the defeat of a culture. Despite the occupation of northern armies, local leaders in the South did not give up hope of attaining autonomy. The Compromise of 1877 that enabled Rutherford B. Hayes of Ohio to become president in return for the withdrawal of the United States military from its occupation of the South affirmed that the dream of an independent culture was not dead. It thereafter became the "Lost Cause," and as such gave shape to a South that had risen anew.

The onset of "Jim Crow" legislation in 1890 gave shape to the "Lost Cause" by putting the formerly enslaved back in what was deemed to be "his proper place," which if not a literal slavery was at least the figurative version of slavery: submission to White Power in the South. When the

Part One—The Regulatory Society

African American leader Booker T. Washington produced the Atlanta Compromise in 1895, it seemed as though African Americans might accept "Jim Crow" if it were made part of a deal in which they were given good schools and justice in the courts. Tom Watson's Democratic Party didn't believe they had to give so much, and they didn't.

Watson was the embodiment of so much that went wrong in the evolving South. He started out as a *Progressive*, or member of the most liberal wing of the Democratic Party He quickly enough discovered that dividing white farmers from black sharecroppers was even better than uniting them in a fight against the seemingly immovable power of the landowners. From there it was only a small step to realizing that electoral success resided in the pleasure taken by small white farmers in the oppression of their black counterparts. Soon enough the Democratic Party was committed to maintaining the racial arrangements of the 1890s.

And soon enough as well the landowners backed such an arrangement because it was in their interest to maintain a cheap labor force on the land. This then was or became the agrarian interest of the South. It amounted to producing inexpensive staples and regaining the antebellum position of *King Cotton* on world markets. To that position was added the fact that the South could lure the textile mills of New England into its hill country by means of the promise of cheap white labor.[1] By the turn of the century, the economy of the new South was defined. It was manufacturing and agrarian, with the latter firmly based on the existence of cheap African American labor on the land.

Even the Ku Klux Klan enjoyed a revival in the wake of Jim Crow. Its popularity was sufficient for it to spread into the North and especially to Indiana in the 1920s. Franklin Delano Roosevelt was the Democratic Party's vice-presidential nominee in 1920. He was relegated to being an observer at a 1924 convention virtually overrun by the Klan, but from that position Roosevelt had a pretty good idea of the party whose leader he would become. Roosevelt had also been Woodrow Wilson's Assistant Secretary of the Navy and so was in a good position to know that Wilson was an unabashed racist.

All of this knowledge was reinforced after Roosevelt contracted polio and spent large periods of time recuperating in Warm Springs, Georgia, which in the mid–1920s he went so far as to make what most called his "second home" and what some even recognized as his preferred first home. Roosevelt's political career may have been in New

1. Democrats and Republicans Before 1932

York state, but his heart was in Georgia and would remain there for the rest of his life. He would even die in Warm Springs, Georgia.

And so the Democratic Party that assumed control of two of the three branches of government in March 1933, was dominated by the South's interest in maintaining the status quo in the all-important area of race relations. This was not merely because Southern legislators, many of them committee chairmen, were racists but was also the case insofar as the agrarian economy of the South required as much. From that position they had some tension with a president seeking to build an alternative foundation for the party in the manufacturing North. Reaching that goal seemed hardly feasible in the first New Deal, or the president's first term in office, and so the new blue-collar basis for the party did not yet appear as a problem.

Shifting the party's base from South to north only became possible in Roosevelt's second term and was only feasible after 1941, in his third term and with a vice president not from the South. There is scant evidence that Roosevelt intended to shift the party's base from South to North, however. More likely is that Roosevelt intended to supplement the party's traditional Southern base with a Northern addition. He was not the first Democratic president to do so. Woodrow Wilson of Virginia had pursued a similar tactic in moving to New Jersey and becoming that state's governor in 1911.[2]

The southern caucus became conscious of its embattled position when in 1945 Harry Truman replaced Roosevelt and began to show sympathy for the predicament of African Americans. Still, such sympathy did not amount to much until Jackie Robinson joined the Brooklyn Dodgers in 1947 and Truman integrated the armed forces in 1948.

Strom Thurmond read the writing on the wall and formed the Dixiecrats in 1948, winning little but showing a growing concern within the party. Truman relied increasingly on the growing strength of Walter Reuther's United Automobile Workers and without yet challenging the South threw his energies into passage of the 1949 Housing Act, the Fair Deal's only legislative victory. By Truman's first elected term, the party was headed away from its southern heritage.

❖❖❖

The decisive shift of the Grand Old Party happened not in the 1870s or 1880s but rather very late in the century, in 1896, and under

Part One—The Regulatory Society

the tutelage of Mark Hanna. To understand Hanna's shift, we do well to skip such panegyrics as Karl Rove's book on William McKinley and the council he received from Mark Hanna and go directly to the source. It has to do with the legal incorporation of American industry.[3] In essence, the move, whether in the form of creating trusts or shifting direct ownership to that of stocks, created well-funded units that corresponded in their scope to a national market. In 1896, Hanna recognized the change and moved toward making corporations the chief source of Republican funding.

After Hanna's move, the Republican Party unequivocally supported Big Business and also concerned itself with cultivating something money could not buy: a popular base. It found this in the aspirations of a lower middle class, including workers divided from each other by skills and organized by the American Federation of Labor (AFL). Hanna's formula worked in 1896 and 1900, was unused in 1904, but was back on track for the 1908 election. It was used again in the 1912 election, and again for the same reason as 1904, which was that Theodore Roosevelt was untrustworthy (no pun intended). In 1920, 1924, and 1928 the party that Hanna had made reasserted itself, his achievement guaranteed by the presence of Andrew Mellon in the cabinet.

The 1932 Republican Party was caught off guard by the remarkable argument of Adolf A. Berle and Gardiner C. Means to the effect that the owners of modern corporations had ceded their property rights by making their companies public.[4] The gist of the argument was remarkably simple: indirect ownership of a corporation (shareholders do not own companies, they own stock in companies, a very different thing) made the owner of shares vulnerable to exploitation by management. The federal government was understood to be obliged to protect property as one of the John Locke's three sanctified rights, hence the federal government had to regulate corporations by compelling them to follow procedural rules like having annual meetings and publishing periodic statements of their activities.

In legal terms, the argument meant that the Democratic Party should cease pursuing a policy of breaking up trusts and should instead regulate them in the public's interest. The earlier policy had led to the Sherman Antitrust Act, the 1911 breakup of Standard Oil, the Pujo hearings, and the storied legal career of Louis Brandeis.[5] This trust-busting essence of the Democratic Party would henceforth give way to regulation.

1. Democrats and Republicans Before 1932

How significant the Berle and Means argument was is difficult to measure because it was expressed through substantive policies. Large corporations agreed or disagreed but were in any case implicated by the National Industrial Recovery Act (NIRA). In this book, a good deal of significance will be assigned to the Berle argument.[6] Berle's argument shifted the focus to accepting the domination of corporations but fencing them in with governmental regulatory powers. The argument enraged Republicans, who viewed the regulation as a direct challenge to the quasi-divine right of property to rule the United States.

Roosevelt listened carefully to Berle's argument, said little, but apparently absorbed much. Six months later Roosevelt was inaugurated president and made the theme of his Inaugural Address the eviction of the moneylenders from the holy temple of American life. Three months later the 1933 Banking Act, better known as Glass-Steagall, was law. It was the first regulatory fence erected by the Roosevelt administration and it set the tone for much else in the New Deal. It did not "bust" the banks as an old Progressive like Brandeis would have Roosevelt do. Instead it instead channeled their behavior, as Berle would have Roosevelt do. There is no more important book for understanding the New Deal than Berle's and Means' *The Modern Corporation and Private Property*.

Berle's book went without saying that General Motors (GM), under pressure to disclose its financial dealing by means of periodic reports made public, would disagree with pressure to recognize the trade unions as bargaining agents for automotive workers and the CIO affiliated UAW as the sole bargaining agent for its workers. But once GM did so in 1937, it then found that the union was amenable to compromise and, if not exactly easy to work with, as least not as difficult as assumed.

Republican opposition to the 1935 Wagner Act giving workers the right to unionize was deeply felt to be a violation of a sacred property right. The precedent remained in this position even when it was shelved during the war. It arose again in the postwar when the UAW immediately went on strike over accumulated grievances. The Republicans won control of Congress in the 1946 midterm election and used their new power to express all the resentment that had been building up during the war. The resentment was real and reached far enough to transcend the limits of the nation state. Both Ford and GM had investments in

15

Part One—The Regulatory Society

Germany that were not dissolved when it declared war on the United States in December 1941. The motivation of both American companies was grounded in the belief that their right to property transcended the limits of national sovereignty.

Republicans were silenced by their minority position in the governments of the time, but that ended in 1946 when the Republicans won control of Congress. The result was the 1947 Taft-Hartley Act loosening and weakening the rights of unions.[7] The main value of the law lay in showing where the Republican mind was in the immediate postwar years.

Insofar as Taft-Hartley was tactical, it was also brilliant. Almost all Southern Democrats joined Republicans in voting to strip labor of powers that had been granted it in the 1935 Wagner Act. The first House vote was 308 to 107, and after the bill was vetoed by President Truman, the second House vote was even more lopsided: 331 to 83. It was this defeat that caused the public to believe that Truman was doomed in the 1948 election.

The main significance of Taft-Hartley was probably cold comfort to Republicans but was nonetheless profoundly significant. Throughout the first and second New Deals, which is to say the first and second Roosevelt administrations, labor unions had reason to hope that the Democratic Party was moving to become a worker's party. So strong was this feeling that the American Labor Party was founded in 1936. It nominated Roosevelt for president and Herbert H. Lehman for governor, mainly in order to test the proposition that New York voters preferred to vote for a labor party candidate than a Democrat. That proposition only made sense in New York City, and even there it did not attract the majority for Roosevelt or even for Lehman, who was much more attractive to the needle trade unions that were behind the American Labor Party.

If the election year 1936 was the high-water mark of the American Labor Party but if it could not even win New York City, then the notion of having the Democratic Party make labor into its main constituency was delusional. When eleven years later the Republicans used Taft-Hartley to demonstrate that even the Democrats would not support strong labor legislation, the idea of a worker's party could be said to be definitively dead.

Taft-Hartley had one other aspect to it that was ominous. In its fine print, it required union leaders to file affidavits testifying that they

1. Democrats and Republicans Before 1932

were not supporters of the communist party nor any other organization seeking the violent overthrow of the United States government. Suddenly the United States was brought back to the Sedition Act of 1918, which was used to convict and imprison Eugene Debs. The way was now cleared for the rise of Senator Joe McCarthy.

2

Glass-Steagall as Foundational Legislation

Carter Glass of Virginia began the year 1933 as dean of the Southern delegation in the Senate. Twenty years earlier, however, and as a young member of the House of Representatives, Glass found himself in a very different position. As a member of the House Banking Committee, he was asked to help author an extraordinarily demanding piece of legislation. It would become the Federal Reserve Act, as brilliant a piece of legislative construction as had been produced in the early 20th century.[1]

Twenty years later, and with a great deal of personal prestige as the financial expert of the Democratic Party, Glass was in position to outdo his former self. The new president needed many things in the spring of 1933, but basic bank legislation was uppermost on his mind, not least because of hearings that had exposed the fraud involved in Wall Street banks using the deposits of small "Main Street" banks for risky investments.[2] Louis Brandeis had complained about such fraudulent activities eighteen years earlier in his book, *Other People's Money and How Bankers Use It*, and now Glass was acting on that complaint.[3]

But where Brandeis wanted to break up the banks, Glass (and apparently Roosevelt) wanted something less, which was to regulate them. Roosevelt first articulated these thoughts in San Francisco in his Commonwealth Club Address of September 23, 1932.[4] The idea for prioritizing regulation had originated with Adolph Berle, a law professor at Columbia University, and mentioned in the previous chapter.[5]

The key to understanding Roosevelt's thinking lay in the distinction

2. Glass-Steagall as Foundational Legislation

between an economy that was growing and one that was settled. In an economy that was growing, outcomes were unknown and no confidence in them could be had. It was for that reason that trust-busting was appropriate. In a mature economy, however, corporate industry was settled, and outcomes were known. Therefore, trusts should be regulated and not "busted." This was Berle's most basic, but by no means his only, rationale for the regulatory state. Now in San Francisco, it was fast becoming Roosevelt's.

When the San Francisco address was finished the evening was over. Roosevelt moved on to different matters, leaving it to others to apply his thinking. One of the others was Glass, who instead of breaking up Wall Street settled for regulating its banks by making them choose between being commercial or investment banks and if they chose the latter, prohibiting them from offering so-called demand accounts.

No measure was more significant than the prohibition on demand accounts, for it created a wall of separation between Wall Street banks and Main Street banks. By not allowing the former to offer demand accounts, federal authorities were telling the latter that they had to earn their money through local business arrangements, like home mortgages. This wall of separation is what gave Glass-Steagall its significance. Other prohibitions were added, but however they were framed, they were not nearly as significant as the prohibition on demand accounts at investment banks.

Such a distinction suited Glass just fine, for as a Southern politician, he was eager to protect the small banks of southern towns from the force of the large banks on Wall Street. Not just that. Glass was also eager to demonstrate Brandeis' point, which was that the power of Wall Street banks was the result of their being able to draw money out of Main Street banks. Glass' partner in authoring the 1933 Banking Act was Congressman Henry Steagall of Alabama, about whom more later, but at this moment it is appropriate to say that Steagall was even more in favor of the wall of separation being created than Glass was.

At this point, the reader would do well to note that the 1933 Banking Act reflected a southern perspective on banking. The loser was Wall Street, located deep in the North, and the winner was Main Street. These antagonistic perspectives were also representative of a divide in America that held the Civil War to be not quite over. There are few more important pieces of legislation in the first third of the 20th century than

Part One—The Regulatory Society

the 1913 Federal Reserve Act and the 1933 Banking Act. Both remind us that the South had the upper hand.

In this chapter I would cover the basic notion of financial regulation, Congressional hearings like the Pujo hearings of 1913–1914 and the Pechora hearings of 1933 and what they revealed, and then conclude the chapter with a final summation of Glass-Steagall and the role in the New Deal it would come to play.

◆◆◆

From the 1880s onwards, the eyes and ears of Progressives were on the physical reality of *corporations* and not so much on those abstract accumulations of money called *banks*. The Morgan bank, for example, was not yet viewed as an actor in its own right. It was a London bank run by an American, Junius Morgan, which had a branch in New York City, run by the son, called by everyone J.P., as in J.P. Morgan. Junius sipped sherry with wealthy British aristocrats, explaining to them how he was able to guarantee high interest rates on their money from typical railroad investments in the United States. The reason was that the British investment was large enough to justify the appointment of a Morgan choice to the railroad's board of directors, and with a Morgan man on the board, the bank felt that it had sufficient control of the railroad. That Morgan man was invariably a vice-president of the New York branch of the Morgan bank, and his task was to ensure that the railroad was run efficiently and profitably.

But why were efficiently run railroads likely to be profitable? The uncomplicated answer was that they were monopolies in their zones of operations, charging local farmers extortionate rates to carry their goods to market, and getting away with it precisely because there was no competition. Occasionally there was a competitor, as for example when an alternative railroad put down tracks in the area in question in order to get a cut of the profits spoken of. But in that case, J.P. Morgan back at 23 Wall Street did not invest in the area's railroads. J.P. was only interested in monopoly control.

And so British capital was systematically sucked out of Britain and absorbed into the development of the American economy, with the latter growing systematically more monopolistic and the British being systematically weakened. To compensate for such a drain, male British aristocrats very often sought to marry American heiresses and thereby cycle some of the money back to Britain, not so much for

2. Glass-Steagall as Foundational Legislation

Britain's sake as for the family's sake (the result was the kind of family Julian Fellowes depicted in the television series *Downton Abbey*, where "Mamma" is an American heiress of Jewish provenance and the Earl of Grantham a well-meaning but feckless British aristocrat). The bank connection back in New York was most likely Kuhn, Loeb, whose chief executive officer was Jacob Schiff, and the railroad—if there was one—was likely way out west. In any case Schiff's investment operation was only a block away from Morgan's, so the details differ but the story's the same.

According to common belief, called upon in Louis Brandeis' collection of essays called *Other People's Money*, the Wall Street banks got money for their investments by paying higher interest rates than local Main Street banks could afford and then investing that money in distant and usually western operations like copper mining, ranching, and of course operating the occasional railroad that would open up a new area of the country. Involved railroads were nearly always given land grants, which they in turn sold to aspiring farmers who would eventually become their customers and unwitting victims. Meanwhile the poor little banks of Main Street were having their money systematically sucked away by the Wall Street's Big Banks.

What (or who) were the Main Street banks? For one, they weren't always located on the Main Streets of towns like fictional Maycomb, Alabama, or Muncie, Indiana. They were sometimes just a short ride on the New York City subway (then a collection of underground railroads). Such was the Knickerbocker Bank on 5th Avenue and 34th Street. Besides being occasionally drained of money by Wall Street banks paying higher interest rates, the Knickerbocker was victimized by panics when depositors thought their bank did not have enough reserves to cover their deposits. In fact, during one such panic in 1907 the Knickerbocker didn't have sufficient reserves, but it did have a telephone and could ring up other banks and make intra-bank loans to cover those deposits. The danger was that such loans might spread the panic rather than stem it, so as often as not a bigger and more persuasive reserve was needed.

This crisis was a matter of savers withdrawing their money from so-called "demand" accounts, which by the nature of that name they were allowed to do. Such accounts were not regulated for the simple reason that there was no banking legislation. Banking was rather a field of activity that fell under the category *laissez-faire*, or the decision that

Part One—The Regulatory Society

the state should not interfere. And so the state, which at the time was the Theodore Roosevelt administration, did not interfere.

Laissez-faire did not prevent other bankers from interfering, however, and so with that in mind, J.P. Morgan stepped into the breach and took command. According to legend, Morgan invited all the city's bankers to his mansion on 36th Street, put them under lock-down in his library, pushed the key into his pocket, and sat outside the library door playing solitaire until they reported they had reached a solution that satisfied the great man. The solution was to have everyone create a reserve fund for the Knickerbocker Bank, a fund so large that nervous savers would cease demanding their money. It worked.

The entire mess with the Knickerbocker Bank might have been avoided if the city's bankers had created a sufficiently large reserve fund in the first place, something that they actually had done a few years earlier when they created an institution called *Bankers Trust*, a bankers' bank dedicated to backing up member banks. Unfortunately for Knickerbocker at the time, it was not a member of that club and so was exposed when a volatile public mood suddenly shifted.

Led by an obscure German-Jewish banker named Paul Warburg and a Columbia University professor of finance named Edwin R.A. Seligman, a number of progressive thinkers began discussions aimed at institutionalizing Morgan's cure for the Knickerbocker. They soon enough caught the attention of Senator Nelson Aldrich of Rhode Island, and after a fact-finding mission to Europe and too many meetings to recall, arrived at legislation that would be signed in December 1913 by Woodrow Wilson and would inaugurate the Federal Reserve banking system.

The final player in the melodrama of creating a national reserve system was Congressman Carter Glass, whose task it was to break a single reserve bank into twelve parts so to mute the complaint that government was controlling the situation. Glass did not broadcast that one of the twelve banks would be located within walking distance of Wall Street and by rules that applied universally would end up holding more reserves than the other eleven banks combined. Carter Glass had to know what he was doing. He was fooling some of the people (those in the South) all of the time into believing that there was no central bank.

The first governor of the New York Federal Reserve was Benjamin Strong. He was experienced not only for having been a Morgan vice-president but also by having been president of Bankers' Trust. To

2. Glass-Steagall as Foundational Legislation

top things off, J.P. Morgan passed away earlier in 1913, and so Strong started his career at the Fed without the old man looking over his shoulder.

Owing to World War I, Benjamin Strong had little to do in the first five years of his tenure, but as a former associate of J.P. Morgan, he may have known the details of the arrangement by which the Morgan bank in New York acted as Britain's financial agent in the United States. Most likely, Strong was sympathetic to the British cause during the war, but his attitude was irrelevant to the larger question of the Morgan bank's activities in acting as Britain's buying agent. Arguably, the Morgan action was troublesome to American interests, but there needed to be a banking law defining it as treason, and no such law existed in the period 1914–1917.

In 1920 Strong befriended Montagu Norman, who had recently been elevated to Governor of the Bank of England. Along with Hjalmar Schacht and Émile Moreau, the four men constituted an informal committee for managing the financial arrangements of the Atlantic world between 1926 and 1929.[6] Add to this list the name of Carter Glass. After acting as Woodrow Wilson's Treasury secretary, Glass became a United States Senator in 1920. He too rose to the top of the financial world in the 1920s.

By staying on the peak of Olympus with Europe's central bankers, Strong became an extraordinarily powerful man. I am breathing rarified air but also neglecting the more compromised air being breathed in by the farmers and store clerks down on the nation's Main Streets. One of them was Congressman Henry Steagall of Alabama. Not nearly as significant as Senator Glass in shaping the 1933 Banking Act, Steagall was still significant for the interests he represented. In the infinite distinctions of the old South, Steagall was not a racist but rather was what might best be called a racial conservative. As such, he was as much at home with working-class African Americans as he was with the white retail clerks and farmers down at the local diner. He knew how to get along and show due respect, and it paid off in wide local support.

Henry Steagall got along, in other words, with the folks on Main Street, or rather on the Main Streets of the multiple towns in his Congressional district. Barbers, hardware store owners, the manager at Woolworth's, car dealers selling Model A's, and yes, presidents of the local savings-&-loan banks were his friends. They met for breakfast at

Part One—The Regulatory Society

the local diner on Main Street where the pick-up trucks were parked in perpendicular spaces outside and their drivers were having eggs over lightly with bacon and grits. If that kind of place existed, which it did everywhere in every town in Alabama's "Black Belt," then Steagall was there every morning having his breakfast.

When Congressman Steagall was in Washington, his business as he saw it was making certain that the small savings banks of his district were not forgotten when it came time to write banking legislation. Henry Steagall's interest in small mom and pop banks is of no great significance in a chapter mainly dealing with Wall Street banks, but it is nonetheless helpful to secure his position now because it helps to explain the contrasting position of Carter Glass and the 1933 Banking Act.

◆◆◆

One of the least expected but most pronounced of the South's traits was its banking tradition, and for two reasons. The first was that the historic South was a predominantly agrarian society, the second that it had a labor supply, the enslaved, who were not only inexpensive but also bound in with its social ways. All of this was remarkably extreme. For example, Virginia had virtually no cities in the 18th century, a fact that entailed it having no large banks and few smaller banks. Virginia was thoroughly agrarian, characterized only by occasional courthouses that gave their names to places, like Appomattox Courthouse or Spotsylvania Courthouse.

It was almost "natural" for Virginia politicians to oppose the creation of any banking arrangements, with the result that Virginia growers were inordinately dependent on British agents called *factors*. These traveling salesmen bought their crops as futures, extending the growers credit that could be used in London and sending ships the following spring to deliver the fine furniture and pick up the tobacco, rice, or cotton. The model for Virginia was that of a Caribbean island that was planted from one shore to the other.

Virginia leaders like Thomas Jefferson and James Madison were not necessarily opposed to small banks at this or that crossroads but were opposed to a privately owned national bank with the financial power to overwhelm local growers and perhaps upset the delicate social relations on the plantations. For that reason, Jefferson and Madison both opposed Alexander Hamilton's first national bank. They succeeded in

2. Glass-Steagall as Foundational Legislation

keeping it out of the Constitution but did not quite have enough heft to keep it out of legislation. The first Bank of the United States (BUS) was given a 20-year lease on life and was authorized to set up operations in Philadelphia.[7]

When BUS's 20-year authorization wound down in 1809, President Madison refused to reauthorize it, letting it die on the vine. Madison then presided as the United States plunged into the War of 1812 with Great Britain. Absent a national bank, he was able to secure adequate financing for the conflict only with the greatest of difficulty. The United States lost all but the last battle of the war and so declared itself the victor. Having learned his lesson the hard way, Madison then concluded his presidency in his seventh state-of-the-union address by requesting authorization for a second BUS. Beginning was the "Era of Good Feelings" and so Congress granted the request. In 1816 the second BUS picked up where the first had left off. It was also limited to a 20-year lifetime.[8]

For a variety of reasons, President Andrew Jackson refused to renew the authorization of the second bank, and so in 1836 the BUS died a second death, and the United States was once again without central banking. Industrialists in Massachusetts took notice and so combined their many accumulations of money into a few banks, of which the leading one was the Suffolk Bank. They proceeded to sustain the textile industry, finance a machine-tool industry, and initiate a leather industry, using hides from California. A lot of this was done by sending second sons west. *West* often meant no farther than western Massachusetts, but just as often it meant the area that would later comprise California, Oregon, and Washington.[9]

All these profitable ventures helped enable the North to win the Civil War, after which it was discovered that the center of banking gravity had shifted from downtown Boston to Wall Street in New York City, where the young J.P. Morgan held sway by having his father recruit British capital to build Western railroads. The direction of growth was almost always north of the Ohio River, and so "Westward Ho!" into Ohio, Michigan, Indiana, Illinois, and the future state of Wisconsin. Everything was financed by Wall Street money concentrated and channeled through J.P. Morgan and a variety of Jewish financiers, among whom were Marcus Goldman and Samuel Sachs. Lehman Brothers, originally from Alabama, financed the movement of cotton, and Kuhn, Loeb cut sufficiently into western railroading to keep J.P. Morgan on his toes.

Part One—The Regulatory Society

All of the money concentrations named above could and were sometimes called "banks," but if that term implied they were regulated, then it was misleading. in fact, there was no bank regulation before World War I and very little after the war. Such a situation enraged "Progressives," the unofficial spokesman for whom was a Boston lawyer named Louis Brandeis. Where Theodore Roosevelt wanted to "bust" the trusts, meaning the incorporated businesses, Brandeis wanted to break up, or "bust," the money concentrations, or banks.

I want to be perfectly clear in what I am saying here. Before World War I, nearly all talk among Progressives was aimed at breaking up the great concentrations of money associated with names like J.P. Morgan, Jacob Schiff, the Lehman Brothers, or Goldman, Sachs. Nearly no talk was aimed at accepting such concentrations but instead regulating them. The idea of regulation seemed to be for others like the railroads[10] or the Chicago stockyards[11] but not for those concentrations of wealth called *banks*. And finally, the campaigns of Louis Brandeis before World War I seemed more directed at the New Haven Railroad than at J.P. Morgan.

The creation of Bankers Trust in 1903 amounted to an admission that such a reserve institution was needed to hold reserves and facilitate its movement to member banks that might be in trouble. The first president was Edmund C. Converse, the second Converse's son-in-law, Benjamin Strong, who remained in the position until he became the first governor of the New York Federal Reserve bank.

No sooner had Benjamin Strong moved into his office than World War I started in earnest. Strong bided his time, complained about how the new Federal Reserve bank was organized, but for the most part wondered about the integrity of the monetary arrangements of the postwar world. The gold standard was a means of controlling the value of any currency pegged to it. That it was overly rigid was demonstrated in the 1890s by J.P. Morgan having to intervene to save the dollar when it turned out the United States did not have the gold reserves to back it.

In the immediate postwar, Strong came to believe that he as governor of the New York Fed could control the value of the dollar by open market sales and purchases of government securities. If the economy was suffering from inflation, Strong would sell government securities. If it was deflating, he would buy, and such action would stabilize the dollar. Strong was exercising what John Kenneth Galbraith later called

2. Glass-Steagall as Foundational Legislation

countervailing power, and it worked just fine. His skill at doing this was first noticed by the British economist John Maynard Keynes in his 1923 *Tract on Monetary Reform*.[12]

It is difficult to know in any detail what Keynes was thinking at the time, but the larger lines of his direction are clear. Keynes believed that the state could intervene with hardly anyone noticing to manage the financial markets. Was he thinking that the state could intervene by fiscal means to manage the entire economy? That we do not know, but that question need not detain us. It was clear in 1923 that the Federal Reserve bank of New York was a regulatory agency, and one with a powerful weapon when it bought and sold with its reserves.

❖❖❖

The main difference between the great Morgan bank on Wall Street and a small savings & loan on Main Street had to do with the capital it accumulated. Neither type of bank wanted to take unnecessary risks. Morgan reduced his by enlarging his capital, and small-town banks reduced theirs by doing credit checks on the locals who wanted loans to build homes for their families.

The great difference between the two was that Morgan could suck up the accumulated capital of the small banks by offering slightly higher interest rates on demand deposits. For the most part, Morgan didn't do this because his father could raise capital in Britain by guaranteeing a high rate of return to aristocrats who agreed to place their capital with Morgan. But others did so, and consequently there was a necessity to regulate them or at least that activity.

Everything said above is fairly obvious, but not so obvious was the argument that the government was legally justified in so regulating banks because any bank's savers were the equivalent of a corporation's stockholders. They rented their money to banks at a fixed rate of return, and the banks in turn invested their money for a higher rate of return. It was all fine as long as everyone understood what was going on and abided by a shared common understanding.

The 1933 Banking Act asked the larger Wall Street banks to make a basic choice between being an investment bank or being a commercial bank. If we are to believe Roosevelt's Commonwealth Club Address of September 23, 1932, the attraction of risky investments was a thing of the past. The United States economy had become a more stable and conservative proposition, and so the big Wall Street banks were likely to

Part One—The Regulatory Society

opt for the commercial designation, choosing to invest their money in established industries like automobile assembly. Roosevelt's bet was that the Wall Street banks would do just that, which for the most part they did.

Glass-Steagall ensured that the smaller banks of Main Street were covered. Their money would no longer be sucked up by Wall Street banks, making them unstable and prone to panic. The way was now clear to create programs involving them.

3

Joe T. Robinson's Home Owners' Loan Act

The 1933 Home Owners' Loan Act embraced the best of small-town America and so embraced a world that was in its twilight when the act was passed.[1] Small-town America was a tightly circumscribed world in which the doctor and the plumber, the carpenter and the bank president, the hardware store owner and the farmer coexisted on equal terms and often even met informally over breakfasts at the local diner. Such venues were scattered across the South and were the mainstay of that region's Democratic Party. They were the essence of *Small-Town* America.

A literary depiction of this America may easily be found in the novel *To Kill a Mockingbird*.[2] Called Maycomb, Alabama, the home of the Finch family was the place where everyone knew everyone else and everyone had his place. The idea of a trial of an African American man for raping or just insulting a white woman was easily imagined since such a prospect had been an integral part of the Jim Crow strategy of the Democratic Party. So strong was the anticipation of such an event that occasionally someone—in the case of Maycomb, a weak-minded white woman—imagined it to have happened. So strong was Jim Crow that convictions were forthcoming even when the evidence to the contrary was as compelling as that presented by Atticus Finch.

Most white working people in such towns owned homes, although usually and only with the help of loans from the local savings bank. For families whose breadwinner worked as carpenter, plumber, electrician, salesman at the local hardware store, or clerk at the bank on Main Street, home ownership meant having social status as well as a roof over the family's head. Hence, home ownership had a psychological dimension that was immeasurable. The idea of losing the family home and

Part One—The Regulatory Society

returning to rental quarters was a terrifying thought, for it meant losing one's friends as well and fending off constant embarrassment when making the rounds on Main Street.

And yet that was precisely what was happening in real world equivalents to places like the fictional Maycomb, Alabama, throughout 1932. True, the stock market crash had happened three years earlier and was by 1932 was a distant memory, but the wave called the Great Depression did not reached places like Maycomb in full force until 1932. The Depression took many forms, but in places like Maycomb, the chief form it took form was at the local savings bank on Main Street.

Home loans in the 1920s had several different names. The one I will use in this and the next chapter is *balloon*, but whatever its name, the logic was everywhere similar. The loan was for a principal amount of money at a specified and fixed rate of interest for a specified time, usually five to seven years. If the breadwinner got lucky at the racetrack, then he paid off the principal and celebrated his good luck. But if he was not so fortunate, which most working men were not, then he dutifully paid the interest every month and after four years and some odd months, made an appointment with the bank manager, and after the usual conversational niceties were exchanged, was told that the loan would be rolled over and another five-year calendar initiated.

The monthly interest payment was a little like rent, but the homeowner didn't see things that way, and so he took the payment as affirmation that he was a respectable citizen of Maycomb and would remain so for as long as he kept meeting his monthly payments.

But in fact the supposed ownership of such a home as our respectable citizen believed was his did not exist, for if our man failed in his payments, the bank would take the home, which was more or less a different way of saying he would be evicted. Of course, this would not happen, for our "homeowner" would rather go without Sunday dinner than fail in his routine payments to the bank. He managed to put aside a little money each week in his sock drawer, and his wife saved her pennies and brought them in rolls to the bank for conversion into paper.

And so the worst nightmare of the homeowner did not come to pass, and it didn't occur to him that any other problem would arise. He therefore felt safe as long as he made his payments and put a little aside every week. It did not occur to him that the bank itself might fail, for

3. Joe T. Robinson's Home Owners' Loan Act

why would the bank if it were getting payments every month from virtually every working man in town?

Bank failure occurred because some people in town, maybe the same ones who had loans, were withdrawing their savings from the bank on Main Street. Who knows why, but if the bank needed to have its loans backed up by savings that were a percentage of the loans and if the bank could not borrow from another bank, then it had no choice but to call in the loans that were coming due, which is another way of saying it would not renew them.

At this point our homeowner might have discovered that his status as *homeowner* was a fiction that he had foisted on himself. He and his family were in fact no different from common, ordinary renters, and so the loss of his home entailed a corresponding loss of status and a return to being an ordinary renter. If our disillusioned homeowner were fortunate, the bank might even rent him the home he had lived in as a "homeowner," only now for a more sizable amount than he had been paying.

If I am correct in this analysis, the representative "homeowner" from Macomb, Alabama, had always been the equivalent of a renter. Previous to the bank's failure, he had rented the money he had been loaned. After the bank's failure in our imagined scenario, he was renting the home with full consciousness.

If we may now return to the real world of 1932 in small towns across the American South, the illusion of homeownership was still intact despite the variety of failures taking shape, personal or institutional failures. Ordinary Americans were complaining to their Congressmen, or if they were not, their Congressmen on their own were finding out the dire straits local citizen-homeowners were in. There was widespread pressure to do something.

❖❖❖

The Home Owner's Loan Act, also known as the Home Owners Refinancing Act, along with the 1933 Banking Act, better known as Glass-Steagall, were passed in the second week of June 1933.[3] Where Glass-Steagall has the names of its sponsors on it, the Home Owners' Loan Act does not. Nonetheless, we know that its author and sponsor was Senator Joe T. Robinson of Arkansas.

Robinson had been Al Smith's running-mate in the 1928 presidential election. He performed better than Smith in the South, which is to

Part One—The Regulatory Society

say, the Democratic ticket performed better in southern than in northern states. It tells a great deal about the Democratic Party that Smith felt he needed to balance his Big City image with that of a down-home, small town figure like Joe Robinson. Roosevelt would do something similar in 1932 with John Nance Garner, remembered today (if at all) for memorably describing the vice presidency as "not worth a bucket of warm piss." Robinson was that type of home-spun politician.

More specifically, Joe Robinson is remembered for two aspects of his personality. The first was his sharp temper and aggressive manner. His nickname, "Scrappy Joe," tells much about the man. His speeches on the Senate floor were invariably invitations to fight, ideally with fists, and then and there. He always wanted a scrap.

To the surprise of everyone else but no one in the Senate, Robinson was also a legislative craftsman who worked over bills put on his desk to ensure they got everything right. The Home Owners' Loan Act was one of the elements of the "Hundred Days," the term given to the first three months after the initial bank holiday had ended, and it got the full attention of Robinson. Most likely it also got the attention of Henry Steagall of Alabama over in the House, perhaps more attention than Steagall gave to the 1933 Banking Act, for Steagall was above all a supporter of the folks "down-home." The bill was tailor-made for Southern and Midwestern populists.

In essence, the bill appropriated federal monies and assigned them to a new agency to distribute as low-interest, long-term loans to qualified applicants, enabling them to pay off those balloon loans from the bank on Main Street and keep their homes on better terms. Making the government loans low-interest was noteworthy, but doubling or tripling their duration to fifteen years was unheard of and more significant. The loans from existing financial institutions were generally for 5 years. By loaning applicants an amount equal to their debt but spreading it over 15 years (and at lower interest), the federal government often made it possible for homeowners in default to pull themselves together and manage at least this aspect of their finances and perhaps all of their finances.

The concept is not new and is still used today by money managers who pull together multiple debts of the same family, make arrangements to double their duration in order to lower the monthly payment, and charge the customer a fee for doing so. In 1933 the Federal government was doing something similar but with only one debt and for

3. Joe T. Robinson's Home Owners' Loan Act

no fee at all. For families with scattered debts and only a vague understanding as to how they had dug such a hole, the federal action was welcome.

The agency created to manage the program was the Home Owners Loan Corporation, or HOLC. The new HOLC was staffed by transferring or borrowing employees from existing federal agencies and putting them in vacant rental quarters in downtown Washington, D.C. That was the gist of the operation. By being so nakedly *ad hoc*, the HOLC gained in enthusiasm what it lacked in efficiency, and since the operation was relatively simple, it accumulated few snarls in the fall of 1933. By mid–October, it was a smooth-running operation.

As is the custom in Washington, D.C., the HOLC was required to file a report at year's end, and from what has been said so far, it might be imagined that the initial year's report would be more interesting than most such routine federal documents. The report was brief, less than thirty pages, but for that still compelling.

At its beginning, HOLC had a mere 87 employees, but the rumor was out that jobs were to be had, and so tens of thousands of persons became interested in employment at the new agency. Given that the agency would also operate out of federal offices in the states, it took months to flesh it out, but it was nonetheless up and running by September of 1933.[4]

The agency let it be known that it was receiving and reviewing applications for aid, which increased in number with each passing month in late 1933. Everything about the review process was routine, which meant that the number of applications by state correlated with the amount of money sent out and so states could be compared. But not always. For example, Michigan residents filed twice as many applications as Massachusetts residents but received only 50 percent more money than did residents of Massachusetts. Unfortunately, it was impossible to determine statistically why this was case.

Matters turned out to be no more revealing in a comparison between Illinois and Indiana. Illinois's population in 1930 was 2.3 times greater than Indiana's, but Indiana residents collectively received 1.25 percent more money than Illinois residents. Why this was the case remains a mystery about which one can now only speculate.

The researcher can speculate on the meaning of these discrepancies, but that meaning, if found or imagined, remains insignificant. More significant are regional differences when one compares clusters of states

Part One—The Regulatory Society

and their applicants. What they show is best illustrated by a comparison between New Jersey, a typical Northern state lodged between New York City and Philadelphia, and North Carolina, as typical a Southern state as any other. New Jersey's population as measured by the 1930 census was slightly over four million at 4,041,334, whereas North Carolina's was somewhat over three million at 3,170, 276, making the Northern state nearly one-third more densely populated than its Southern counterpart in this comparison. Yet when it came to number of applicants, North Carolina far outstripped New Jersey, with 375 as opposed to 224 applicants receiving $1,292,906 as opposed to $973,1181, or about thirty percent more dollars.

What did this prove, or at least support, in an argument? To be perhaps too hasty about the matter at hand, I think the evidence supported the contention that the Home Owners' Loan Act would have more constituents in the Southern and Midwestern states and arguably more in agrarian than in industrial states.[5] How much that argument mattered depended on where the Roosevelt administration went next.

If the administration continued the logic of the Home Owner's Loan Act, it would find new and more creative ways to support an already existing small-town America. In 1933, such a direction was highly likely for the new administration in Washington, for though the president was technically from New York state, his chief support was from the southern states, and if the representatives of those states were in only questionable control of both houses of Congress, they were by dint of the seniority rule certainly in control of leadership positions in Congress. Southern legislators would easily control the legislation making its way through Congress, and furthermore they were conscious of this as a social obligation of theirs.

Much talk was given to the *Lost Cause* of the Confederacy, but the cause of Jim Crow arrangements in the agrarian South was not yet a fully lost cause in the 1930s. If the thuggery associated with it could be brought under control, it could be made to last indefinitely. The small-town South of *To Kill a Mockingbird* was very much alive in 1933.

❖❖❖

In this chapter I am trying to make my way through a narrow corridor between the full creation of the 1933 Home Owners' Loan Act and the 1934 Housing Act, mainly for the purpose of seeing how the earlier

3. Joe T. Robinson's Home Owners' Loan Act

law influenced the later legislation. Fortunately we are given the kind of judgment that rings true in the first annual report of the law's administrative agency, the HOLC. It concluded by noting that the

> ...people are making a wonderful effort to pay according to their contract, illustrating the truth that a man will go to the limit of his strength to hold his home. Each loan made represents a mortgage on that particular spot which some family calls home, and it represents toil, sacrifice, and love.[6]

The spirit is sentimental but was most likely genuinely felt. The first item to note is the emphasis on contract between citizens and government, for social conservatives the ideal way of arranging public affairs. Secondly, however maudlin, at the time there was a certain truth to the claim that home ownership was the distinguishing form of property ownership in a bourgeois society, even one located in the fictional Maycomb, Alabama.

If Karl Marx was correct in his description of proletarians as people with nothing to lose, then the description of the first HOLC Annual Report about a man going to the limit of his strength to hold his home is probably of social significance. The description is accurate in respect to distinguishing an AFL member from a prospective member of the CIO, of workers from mere laborers. This is not only to say that AFL members were terrified of being recognized as prospective CIO members. It was also to say that prospective CIO members would long for that species of property that would identify them as from a higher social order, namely, the AFL.

These distinctions are too ambitious and so should be taken with a grain of salt. Not at all too ambitious, however, is any claim to the affect that the Home Owners' Loan Act was a model for the forthcoming 1934 Housing Act. It was this in a concrete and also more abstract sense.

The concrete sense had to do with doubling the duration of loans to working people. The claim of small and local lending agencies was that they could not afford to lend for more than 5 to 7 years. Whatever one thinks of that claim, it was not much disputed. The government thought that it had greater longevity than the average S&L and so could more than double the duration of any loan, thereby halving the monthly fee and easing the lives of ordinary Americans in the dire circumstances of 1933. No one quarreled with this move. It was taken to be little short of brilliant.

Part One—The Regulatory Society

The abstract sense of the 1933 HOLC being a model for the 1934 Housing Act had to do with completing the project begun by Henry Ford in late 1913 of replacing skilled workers with unskilled laborers by giving them secure jobs on the assembly line and encouraging them to cease being proletarians and take their place as proper bourgeois citizens of the republic. By this reckoning, the 1934 Housing Act promised to be the threshold into the consumer society of the future.

4

The 1934 Housing Act and "Redlining"

Today few people know of the 1934 activities of Winfield Riefler, but in that year at least one significant visitor to Washington, D.C., appreciated the work of the obscure economist.[1] The visitor was John Maynard Keynes, not yet famous as the creator of Keynesianism but well-known because of his 1919 book attacking the Versailles peace settlement. Before departing for home, Keynes sent Riefler a note on hotel stationary.

Mayflower Hotel—20/5/34

Dear Riefler,

You may be interested to see the enclosed from the Times *of May 17 about a project (still far from national) for a national scheme to build working class houses to rent in England. It would be a grand thing if you could add something of the sort to your own scheme.*

I was up at the Senate yesterday and did what little quiet propaganda I could for your brilliant bill—especially with Senator Barkley[2] with whom I had a good talk about it and whose doubts I endeavored to dispel. I hope you have good luck with it.

I am leaving Washington today after one of the most crowded and fascinating experiences of my life. I envy you all!—but your real job will come after you have achieved victory.

Yours sincerely, JM Keynes[3]

From his conversations with Riefler, Keynes had taken away the idea of building a government program around the financial instrument of self-amortizing debt, more commonly called *the mortgage* or better still, *the home-mortgage.* The term is derived from the French word for death, *morte*, which in the financial world refers to a loan, the principal of which is paid down alongside its interest until both are "dead."

37

Part One—The Regulatory Society

The alternative is a species of loan in which the debtor mainly pays interest but may pay down the principle as well. Such loans include the risk of putting the borrower into a permanent state of debt, something that Riefler wanted to avoid in the bill. Balloons are retired only by borrowers who are disciplined enough to separately save an amount equal to the principal, a difficult task most of the time

Because self-amortizing loans were the outstanding aspect of Riefler's thinking, my guess is that they were what Keynes was referring to when he commented on "your brilliant bill." The fact that Keynes actually lobbied for the bill to Senator Barkley suggests how deeply impressed he was by the concept of the self-amortizing loan and Riefler's proposed use for it.

Notable in Keynes's note is his mention of rental housing for workers in Britain. I'm not quite certain what Keynes was referring to since Council housing with rental quarters had been offered to workers on a large scale since the period immediately after World War I, but Keynes was impressed and so may have considered home ownership valuable as an option to renting.

But did the British economist think at all about the prospect of ownership as the sole means of obtaining worker housing? We shall not know because Keynes doesn't tell is in this note or elsewhere.

Here in Keynes' note is, if I may say so without further proof, one of the great problems of class relations at the time. Working classes everywhere were conventionally thought of as occupying rental housing because that sort of housing matched their status as expendable elements of the production process. Making the working class, or at least workers, into homeowners by means of a clever financing device was thought to be interesting by Keynes ("*your* brilliant *bill*"), but did Keynes grasp that such a move would put the working class on the road to becoming a middle class and that such a move was problematic? Again, we don't know, and Keynes was writing a note and not one of his treatises, and so we shall never know.[4]

For his part, Riefler might easily have been drummed out of Washington with the rest of the Hoover administration had he not undergone an intellectual conversion by grasping the futility of the Hoover administration's approach to finances.[5] What in fact saved Riefler was something else: he was employed by the Federal Reserve Bank and so was technically not a part of the Hoover administration. So while the Hoover loyalists were cleaning out their desks, Riefler was still working from

4. The 1934 Housing Act and "Redlining"

his. Riefler wiled away the end-time of the Republican order by writing a book.[6] Eventually, he jumped ship from the Fed and reemerged in the new Roosevelt administration. There he became one of four members of Roosevelt's Committee on Housing.

In 1934, Winfield Riefler wrote an *aide memoire* in which he expounded on his understanding of the financial situation in the previous decade, which is to say, the period dominated by Republican presidents. His thinking is not earth-shattering, but the *aide memoire* does have the singular advantage of revealing that Riefler was capable of drawing back from the present and its immediate pressures for the sake of a long-term perspective. What follows is Riefler's depiction of the crisis confronting the President's Committee on Housing:

> *The mortgage money market in this country has never been organized along sound lines calculated to stand up under economic pressure. Very few mortgages are made on an amortization basis by which the debtor is required to retire a fixed proportion of the principal annually out of the income on the property, and the mortgage is outstanding until it is fully paid. Instead, most American mortgages are drawn for 3 or 5 years without provisions for amortization or curtailment of principal.*
>
> *This means, first, that there is no provision for automatically extinguishing mortgage indebtedness out of the income on mortgaged properties, and, secondly, that a huge volume of mortgages becomes legally due each year which cannot possibly be paid off except by refunding. If they become due in a period of uncertainty, such as that which has prevailed since 1930 when new mortgage money is scarce, they cannot be refunded, the mortgage market becomes utterly demoralized, and debtors over a wide area of the market find themselves subject to immediate foreclosure and a prey to unscrupulous financial tactics.*[7]

The first thing to notice has to do with Riefler's use of the term *mortgage*. Riefler uses the term generically as a synonym for *loan*, by which I mean a loan of any type. This raises the question whether Riefler was sloppy or simply corresponding to the common usage of the time. It is easy but mistaken to conclude the former. More likely Riefler was actually writing clearly about a term that had not yet been disaggregated. Despite the resultant confusion, it is evident that Riefler knows what he is talking about.

Riefler began by posing what is today called a *stress test* in respect to the typical home-financing of the 1920s. He found such loans wanting because they lacked a desired equilibrium. Credit was extended in the form of 3 to 5 year "mortgages" without any provision for retiring the accrued debt. Instead there was a mystifying process called "refunding," meaning an agreement by the bank to "roll-over" the loan.

But "roll-overs" are potentially deadly to the homeowner. They work fine in good times but fail under the kind of financial stress that had prevailed since 1930, when bankers express the utmost concern but unfortunately have to tell the client to pay up the full amount of the loan or the bank will be forced to repossess the family home. Out of this came the "utter demoralization" that Riefler spoke of, followed by "unscrupulous financial tactics," most likely meaning the hard-money men, and if a deal can't be struck with the latter, then come the "thugs," much like in the countryside of India.

Riefler's comments serve well to demonstrate his understanding in 1934. He valued an *equilibrium* model, by which he meant an equation that incorporated all extant factors into a model that didn't fail. The current "balloon" model did not do that. That balloon loans cannot be refunded in bad times may be considered a function of the economic cycle, but ordinary Americans ought to be put into a position where they can ride out system failure and not be utterly demoralized, foreclosed, and so weakened that they are subject to unscrupulous financiers.

To use a metaphor to describe Riefler's thinking, if I am asked to build a sailboat capable of crossing the Caribbean, I will include in the design a deck, which on boats is like a Tupperware lid on a storage container. In an impending storm, the boat can then be entered through a hatch that can be secured from the inside, thereby making the boat into a watertight unit.

To not include such a deck is also possible, but then the resultant sailboat is not watertight and so dare not stray far from the shore for fear that it will be swamped in any storm worth the name. Riefler saw the existing home-loan system as something like a deckless sailboat that in the early 1930s had been caught out in the midst of a Shakespearean tempest. It was not made to survive any kind of storm and most likely would not survive what Milton Friedman and Anna Jacobson Schwartz called *The Great Contraction*.[8]

Again, we are forced to confront the question of rental housing versus home ownership for the working class, a question I expanded on a few pages earlier in a footnote of the issue. Such questions—rental vs. owned housing for workers—are missing in Winfield Riefler's sphere of discourse.

◆◆◆

4. The 1934 Housing Act and "Redlining"

Nonetheless, Winfield Riefler was a Keynesian before that term became fashionable. He subscribed to comprehensive government coverage of all phases of the economic cycle, not just the *ups* like the 1920s, but also the *downs* of the early 1930s not just the good years, but also the bad ones. He understood the defect of not intervening, that a lack of such action would cause "utter demoralization" followed by "unscrupulous financial tactics." No wonder that Keynes was fond of Riefler. No wonder Keynes lobbied for his bill.

A year earlier, Riefler had written another *aide memoire*, apparently again with himself imagined as its lone reader. In this one, he also made known his canny grasp of the financial arrangements of the 1920s:

> *Our object should be to create conditions under which a natural and free market for mortgage money will spring up and to consider the use of Government funds in this connection only in the sense of helping to provide an example which the private market might follow. I think we should consider the drafting of a federal mortgage company incorporation law which would permit private capital to incorporate in model federally examined mortgage companies which would be subject to conditions of examination and operation designed to prevent those flagrant financial abuses which have demoralized the mortgage market in the past.*[9]

Perhaps even ahead of Keynes, Riefler was imagining how the government might play a constructive role in an economy dominated by accumulated capital. Riefler imagines a law that would allow private money to incorporate in *model federally examined mortgage companies*, as clumsy a phrase as Riefler was ever to create. There is no reason these may not be already existing local financial institutions like building societies or savings-and-loans. In that case, the key was to make sure that they were *federally examined*.

I am unable to determine how aware Riefler was of the thinking of Adolf Berle and Gardiner Means, who argued that the federal government was within its constitutional powers in examining and regulating corporations because the latter were not (or were no longer) private property.[10] Before Berle and Means, Louis Brandeis had argued a similar argument in respect to banks in *Other People's Money*, and Riefler might well have invoked Brandeis' argument in respect to local savings institutions, for they systematically profited from other people's money.[11] But Riefler was no constitutional lawyer and so he did not argue such arguments.

Part One—The Regulatory Society

Riefler tends to write run-on sentences that beg to be broken-down to be more clearly understood. The first sentence above might better read: *The government should create the legal conditions [pass laws] under which a free market for mortgage money will grow naturally.* Riefler is evidently proposing the creation by the state of a market for mortgage brokers, including local financial institutions. Then to reinforce the point: *Consider the use of government funds only to provide an example which the private market might follow.* Again, a mortgage broker is being imagined, one in which government funding is meant as the model.

Riefler knew what the financial instrument called a *mortgage* was and wanted to fit it to the longing of ordinary Americans for a home as a symbol of their salvation in what was otherwise a Shakespearian tempest. Riefler's problem was then the financing of home mortgages. That was what the first sentence above referred to: *The government should create the legal conditions [pass laws] under which a free market for mortgage money will grow naturally.*

Winfield Riefler was by no means the inventor of the home mortgage. Riefler was rather something else more significant. Riefler was the man who grasped that the rules of the market needed to be used as tools and, presumably, if they were, the market would accommodate ordinary Americans. That the ordinary assembly line worker was capable of becoming a homeowner if the finances of the purchase were organized around the principle of the self-amortizing debt is perhaps too much to impose on Riefler's thinking, but it is difficult to guess what else he was thinking. This was after all *The New Deal*, and more ambitious schemes were being proposed every day.

There is no evidence that Riefler intended to create a mechanism for launching the consumer society. Few economists thought this way before World War II.[12] Indeed, such thinking would seldom be the case before 1950. It was only retrospectively that one could envision what was in 1934 still an unlikely outcome.

Finally, there is Riefler's precise depiction of the 1934 understanding of the market for home loans. It reads like total confusion but is actually an accurate depiction of the state of conceptualization at the time. There was no sharp distinction between a mortgage and a balloon loan, and hence there were opportunities to conflate the two terms and confuse the applicant, who for our purposes is posited to be an unskilled blue-collar worker. The market so depicted by Riefler's vocabulary was

4. The 1934 Housing Act and "Redlining"

a matter of smoke-and-mirrors, or rather a market in which the dictum *caveat emptor* applied more than ever.

Such was the conceptual vocabulary of the day. Riefler had the intention to change it through the simple device of government guarantees. By that means, participants in the market would be compelled to change their vocabularies. If the government guaranteed home mortgages capable of full amortization, then the term *mortgage* would enter the common vocabulary. If the government guaranteed *fixed rates*, then adjustable rates might be offered but would have a different or less risky attraction. In such circumstances, *balloons* would clearly appear to be the kind of credit traps they were, for only the most gullible would believe that they could voluntarily save an amount equal to the principal in the five or so years given to pay off the loan.

※ ※ ※

If a 21-year-old just out of college finds an apartment and is eager to sign a lease, the agent may agree but do so only on condition that the parents guarantee the lease with their signature and their credit-rating. The 21-year-old may have no credit rating, not because he or she doesn't spend money but rather because he or she did not spend it in the right way, which is by means of a credit card. The advantage of the latter device is that it generates a measure called a *credit-rating*.

In 1933 there were no credit cards (as we know them). It does not follow, however, that one had no "credit rating" in the substantive sense of that term. If one had graduated from Harvard or Yale, one had also an informal "credit rating" that might lead to a position at Goldman, Sachs or the like. If one was a skilled carpenter with references, then one had a credit rating of a different sort, 1933 style. Credit ratings have been around for a long time, only without the label.

Apparently, Winfield Riefler understood the problem and was willing to use the government's good name, as established by Alexander Hamilton in his First *Report on the Public Credit* to Congress in 1790.[13] Playing the role of Hamilton, Riefler would have the government guarantee loans made to a class of homebuyers who were worthy but with no accompanying credit-rating. The group was not made up of Harvard or Yale graduates or skilled carpenters or electricians. It was rather made up of unskilled laborers who were at the time being organized on an industrial basis by a new species of union dissatisfied with the AFL. Riefler had confidence that such laborers were good credit risks, and so his

Part One—The Regulatory Society

most basic impulse was to give them the closest thing he could imagine to a positive credit rating.

Admittedly, the above argument is speculative, but it is hard to know what else Riefler was thinking if not what I am suggesting. Who else could Riefler have been thinking of if not the large and identifiable cohort of unskilled assembly-line workers in factories run by Ford, General Electric, Firestone Tires, Youngstown Sheet and Tube, Inland Steel, General Motors, or the massive United States Steel Corporation then being unionized by John L. Lewis? There was no plausible alternative. Riefler was making an analysis of the American economy in 1934 and tailoring a program keyed to an identifiable group deemed by Riefler to be worthy of a credit rating: unskilled assembly line workers.

There is nothing radical about such an analysis. In fact, very much to the contrary, it had been growing in persuasive power for the previous 20 years before Riefler participated in it. What I described above was roughly what John L. Lewis was thinking every day, what Samuel Gompers's successors at the head of the AFL were worried about, and what Antonio Gramsci celebrated as *Fordismo*.[14] It was the rise to prominence of the unskilled laborer.

Everything said or claimed above is in harmony with Roosevelt's speech to the San Francisco Commonwealth Club in September 1932. For if the economy was settling down to a period of stability after a period of wild growth, then so too was the working class settling down in the sense that unskilled workers with no stability in their lives were being given stability in the form of steady jobs on some assembly line. Indeed, the underlying notion of *assembly* as opposed to *making* carries with it the notion of the widespread stability of a supply chain snaking out from Detroit to cities like Toledo, Akron, Youngstown, Pittsburgh, and Cleveland. The United States had changed, and Roosevelt understood that.

❖❖❖

The tone of my analysis in Chapter 2 was that President Roosevelt might also have thought this way and therefore given serious consideration to the concept of *limited equity*, which was a concept of ownership tailored to the solidarity of the organizing laboring class. I am not the only observer to assign a radical significance to the fact of the Amalgamated Housing Cooperative in the Bronx.[15] Roosevelt was well aware that

4. The 1934 Housing Act and "Redlining"

the concept of limited equity was of critical significance to the cohort of workers culturally attuned to it.

Housing an increasingly disciplined set of unskilled workers was central to the continued smooth functioning of the industrial economy that was emerging, but that was not the only concern of policymakers. The threat of class-revolution had peaked in 1917 and plateaued over the next five years. Thereafter it receded, but worker revolution remained a concern even after Lenin adopted the NEP for the Soviet Union.

Politicians and policy makers continued to respond with policies meant to counter revolutionary fervor by building adequate worker housing. In the United States, that kind of policy making continued nowhere more than in New York state, where Governor Smith was willing to accommodate social democratic operations like the Amalgamated Clothing Workers of America of Sidney Hillman. As a major figure in New York state in the 1920s, Franklin Roosevelt knew of all this.

So why didn't Roosevelt push for limited equity housing in 1934, when the first housing act for workers was being conceived by Winfield Riefler? A national housing policy aimed at a group as significant as blue-collar industrial workers was a major moment in United States history, certainly more major than most New Deal policy moments. So why didn't Roosevelt push for limited equity housing modeled on the Amalgamated houses in the Bronx?

The president did in fact move in the direction I am describing when he supported the Resettlement Administration and the creation of "green' suburbs by a key member of his administration: Rex Tugwell,[16] There is nothing so remindful that the ideas of Congresswoman Alexandria Ocasio-Cortez, better known by her initials as AOC," especially her notion of a *Green New Deal*, are not at all new. Rex Tugwell of Columbia University was the AOC of his age, and he was this in housing as well.

There were several such suburban towns—Greenbelt, Maryland, Greendale, Wisconsin, Greenhills, Ohio, and Jersey Homesteads, New Jersey, the name of which was later changed to Roosevelt, New Jersey.[17] All of them are especially interesting, but the last named Jersey Homesteads is the most interesting because it entailed the resettlement of Jewish garment workers from New York. So-called "Jersey Homesteads" was the closest thing to limited equity housing sponsored by the New Deal administration. It was meant to be a continuation or extension of the Amalgamated homes in the Bronx, which were built at the edge of Crotona Park in the Bronx to give it the desired "green" setting.

Part One—The Regulatory Society

But despite the "green" intentionality installed by Tugwell, "Jersey Homesteads" eventually failed to attract and hold the president's allegiance. The reason had to do with the kind of support it failed to include. Tugwell's program was purely governmental, or rather purely a matter of state action, and Roosevelt was unready for this. Indeed, as far as I can make out as a researcher, the 1934 Housing Act is the first significant instance in United States history of this approach being taken by the Democratic Party. But let me cease being overly involved in abstractions and provide some illustration,

At its core, the 1934 Housing Act was about financing, not housing, and so we might fail to understand it properly until we grasp that the legislation as drafted was also meant to recruit the support of the nation's savings-and-loan institutions, commonly called S&Ls. Glass-Steagall's elements were meant to throw up a barrier to Wall Street banks but without changing anything else, the business of home mortgages had to remain with or even revert to local banks. Roosevelt was unwilling to go the whole way and make the state the source of funding for home construction.

❖❖❖

Besides this kind of abstract calculation of political support, there is also the persistent fact that the Roosevelt administration's New Deal was in 1934 still based predominantly on southern support. Just as there was little experience of trade unions in the agrarian South, so too there was little experience of centralized banking. Any failure to include the South's Main Street institutions entailed risking overall failure of the legislation.

Not only small banks, however, but also real estate developers were within the range of being appealed to by the authors, presumably Winfield Riefler first of all, of the 1934 legislation. That their inclusion may have been an afterthought is helpful in indicating the extent to which the authors of the legislation had do make up their script as then progressed. In 1936, FHA administrators produced a vision of a model home keyed to conventional American middle-class tastes. *Technical Bulletin No. 4* of the new FHA, called "Principles of Planning Small Houses," set the stage for the construction that started a little more than ten years later in Levittown.[18] If there was a housing counterpart to the Model T Ford, it was the home depicted in sketches in *Technical Bulletin No. 4*.

4. The 1934 Housing Act and "Redlining"

The vision had earlier been made an aim of the so-called *Sociological Department* of the Ford Motor Company. In 1913, Henry Ford had opted for the Five-Dollar day not because he was generous but rather because that was what he deemed to be the minimum wage needed by a family of four living in a tidy two-bedroom cottage. In 1913, the majority of Ford's assembly line workers were foreign-born, and if they weren't yet heads of nuclear families, that was nonetheless what Mr. Ford wished for them. So powerful was the vision that the company treated employees as families and not individuals.[19]

The ideal was a detached home, but from what can be made out, the home appears to still be in the city, which in Detroit was entirely possible. Ten years later, as depicted by the Federal Housing Authority, the home had been expanded and moved to a location outside the city, one with lawn and trees and a garage to hold a Ford Model A.

The details need not distract us. Significant is the home as a phenomenon, which is to say, a material realization of a popular mental image. Any prospective buyer would immediately see that the family could easily be expanded by two or three children by developing the attic of the house. There is no way into the basement because there was no basement. The foundation was a poured slab of cement, typical of homes built in Arizona but virtually unknown in the wet and cold northeast.[20]

During the same period described above, author James Truslow Adams published the book in which he coined the term "The American Dream."[21] Adams was one of the most popular narrative historians of the interwar period, and so one can be confident that his term had widespread appeal and influence.[22] The meaning Adams attached to the term was upbeat and positive, perhaps best captured in his admonition that in life all of us had to learn how to earn a living and live a life. Adams separated the two modes of education because he was not entirely confident that Americans would be up to realizing the dream he described in his book. He was correct, but not for the reasons he imagined.

❖ ❖ ❖

A troublesome aspect of the 1934 Housing Act was that Americans would be so enamored of their home that they would easily exaggerate threats posed to it by alien forces. Nowhere was this more apparent than in the literary comment accompanying the residential security maps published by HOLC and adopted by the FHA. Every aspect of their vocabulary is cast in the image of alien forces invading and threatening the new suburbs. Hence, defense mechanisms are urged, such as seeing to it that a park or wooded area or perhaps a highway separates the valued property from alien, invading forces. It was not a great step to imagine that the alien invaders were African Americans, and that the perceived risk they posed was the cherished value at the center of the hope for suburbs, namely, property values.

Naturally, none of this happened in the 1930s.[23] This was not because residents dismissed the threats as meaningless but rather because very few if any African Americans had the wherewithal to get near the new suburbs. Not just that, there were fewer suburbs in the mid–1930s than there would be in the mid–1950s and succeeding decades. Nonetheless, the elements of a distinctly American fascism were laid down with the 1934 Housing Act. All that was now needed were the elements to bring them to life.

All of these elements of the 1930s add up to the elements of a nascent American Fascism without the glue to weld them into a single, coherent movement. Missing was the size and scope of the suburbs, the reality of a threat from African Americans, and the presence of a leader like the fictional Berzelius "Buzz" Windrip to put the elements all together. What amazes about the early 1930s is the presence of so many prophetic voices, led by Adams. The issue it poses will return to us in later chapters dealing with the working class.

The 1934 Housing Act inherited and accommodated the color-coded risk-assessment maps that included the color red, as in the term *red lining*. The practice came to the 1934 legislation from the 1933 Home Owner's Loan Act. It was part of southern *Jim Crow* practices long before 1933. Any question about Congress resisting such a practice was close to being absurd, so the only meaningful question had to do with whether the president would exert any influence to resist such racism.

The answer is no, but more significantly, the explanation continues to be that Roosevelt was in his first term and so unsure of his party political base.[24] He saw himself as inordinately dependent on the South and certainly more dependent than he would be when northern industrial labor got organized, which it wasn't in 1934.

◈◈◈

4. The 1934 Housing Act and "Redlining"

The older of the two species of unionization existent in 1934, the American Federation of Labor, reflected the life of small-town America and so was very much a creature of the 19th century imagination. Work in this imagining was still an intact and complex activity, meaning that its product—always complex—was the outcome of individual effort. The mind-set of AFL leaders remained fixated on such individual effort well into the 20th century, as if the world of work had not changed.

The shift from 19th to 20th century revolves about the greater reorganization of work from crafts taking place in a workshop under the aegis of a master to labor taking place in ever larger factories in which even the notion of *craft* was becoming absurd. The latter mutation did not begin happening with melodrama until Henry Ford reorganized his operations at Highland Park by creating the moving assembly line and the Five-Dollar Day. It culminated when Highland Park was left behind for the River Rouge plant in the 1920s.

The notion that labor unions were dangerous and revolutionary whereas ownership and management was harmlessly conservative was in the 1920s one of those myths that persisted only on the basis of widespread gullibility. The truth was that management was utterly revolutionary and that labor unions like the AFL were slow to pick up on the gathering change.[25] This was why John L. Lewis of the United Mine Workers was so critically important. He fully recognized what was happening and urged his fellow AFL leaders to get ahead of the curve of change and recognize the need to organize on an industrial basis (by industry) rather than on a craft basis.

The reorganization of labor would eventually follow suit, but in the United States that didn't happen until after the Flint Sit-Down strike of General Motors in the spring of 1937. That event took place in Roosevelt's second term, and even then the president would not grow confident of his new base until the final year of his second term. Once World War II started in earnest, only then was did Franklin Roosevelt begin to recognize the significance of the change that was brought about with the creation of the embryonic United Auto Workers (UAW). Only then would Roosevelt begin thinking the tabooed thought that the Democratic Party had added North to South as its basis. Only in 1940 would Roosevelt feel confident enough to drop John Nance Garner as his running mate and let an unsettled party choose Henry A. Wallace as his vice president.

◈ ◈ ◈

Part One—The Regulatory Society

For the industrial working class, the 1934 Housing Act put the question of spending on an even plane with that of saving. But would the industrial working class actually spend? Blue-collar men allowed themselves a bit of bluster to demonstrate to themselves that they were heads of families, but housewives counted every penny down to the hour when those small brown pay-envelopes arrived on Friday afternoons. As of 1934 there was no consumerist ethic in the blue-collar working class.

The solution to this dilemma was remarkably easy and if we judge by the speculations in Riefler's papers, understood perfectly well by the author of the legislation. Like magic, Riefler's solution was to make spending into a species of saving, thereby averting the problem entirely. If a representative blue-collar family was to finance a home that complied with the recommendations of *Technical Bulletin No. 4*, he (and it was a *he*) would spend the next 360 months of his life (that was 30 years) saving to meet the monthly mortgage requirement. Here in a nutshell was Winfield Riefler's genius: he had induced a nation of savers to become consumers by persuading them that they were in fact saving.

But what if Charlie Chaplin's job on the assembly line as depicted in *Modern Times* had left Charlie without his weekly pay envelope? Here Riefler could depend on blue-collar Charlie's imagined reasoning: the worst that could happen would be the loss of Charlie's mortgaged home, but the same fate awaited Charlie with a rented tenement in Brooklyn. Charlie would have been no worse off buying than renting, and with any luck, he would have been better off buying.

I have no evidence that blue-collar workers thought that way in 1934, but certainly there is evidence that Brooklynites thought that way in 1947 when visiting "Island Palms" on Long Island to consider renting one of Bill Levitt's homes.[26] Multiple visitors told Levitt that they would prefer purchasing than renting the home they were looking at.[27] Levitt soon enough got the idea and shifted from rentals to sales. Immediately commitments picked up. Consumers understood that under the still existing 1934 Housing Act's terms, they were saving by buying.

But that was 1947 and not 1934, but even though the earlier argument crafted by Winfield Riefler was powerful, it was not enough to tip the scales and launch a consumer revolution. Unemployment was too recent a memory, the 10 percent down payment requirement was still

4. The 1934 Housing Act and "Redlining"

a real obstacle for blue-collar workers living pay-envelope to pay envelope, and the savings "overhang" accrued by women working in defense industries was completely lacking. The latter group was a precondition of the postwar consumer society, and they were not present in the prewar.

5

Wagner-Steagall and Public Housing

Federally financed and built public housing originated in 1933 under the aegis of the National Industrial Recover Act.[1] Its implementing agency was Harold Ickes's Public Works Administration (PWA).[2] The two projects competing for the honor of being the first were the *Techwood Homes* in Atlanta, Georgia, and the *First Homes* on New York City's East Village. They served as models for further construction, but federal agencies were slow to act and were in any case undermined by the Supreme Court declaring the program in violation of the 10th Amendment and so unconstitutional.[3] The court directed that public housing was a power reserved to the states and that future construction had to be directed through state agencies.

Prior to the ruling, only one state, New York, had formed an agency to involve the state in such construction. *NYCHA*, or the New York City Housing Authority was formed in 1934 and indicated by its existence that New York State authorities thought that the need was in New York City, at least more than in the greater state, and so agreed that New York City would have its own housing authority.[4]

At this point, it is necessary to lay down an understanding not readily available to a 21st century observer. In the mid–1930s, New York City was the site of the most systematic and chronic poverty in the United States. Until 1924 and passage of a restrictive immigration act, immense numbers of immigrants from Eastern and Southern Europe had entered New York City. Some of the immigrants continued on to the Upper Midwest, but most stayed on in the city and settled in its Lower East Side, making it the nation's most notorious slum.

The city responded by regulating housing or approving housing built by one or another of the needle trade unions. The best known was

5. Wagner-Steagall and Public Housing

the Amalgamated Housing in the Bronx, sponsored as a limited equity project by the Amalgamated Clothing Workers of America and its chief, Sidney Hillman. The project was put in the hands of Abraham E. Kazan, who viewed the Bronx project as a model for future workers' housing in New York City.

Housing sponsored by unions was meant for union members, who were for the most part second generation Jews whose parents had migrated from the Pale of Settlement before World War I.[5] Such exclusivity irritated other social groups, leading to sub rosa criticism and occasionally outright opposition. It was in such a context that NYCHA was formed in 1934 to manage public housing projects and ensure social equity.

Everything would have been complicated enough had it not been for the shadow of the president of the Long Island State Parks Commission hovering over New York City. Robert Moses entered the City big time in 1933 with a proposal to build the Triborough Bridge and all of its access roads. The mayor in 1934 was Fiorello La Guardia. He admired Moses and wanted to involve him in city affairs, specifically in building housing and developing parks.

The most significant project La Guardia involved Moses in was in the clearance of so-called slum housing between 14th and 20th Streets on the east side as well as the construction of thousands of apartments intended for veterans of World War II. Called *Stuyvesant Town*, the immense venture was at the very least a model for other public housing, not just for the city but also for other cities in similar circumstances.

But Stuyvesant Town was not just a model for public housing. It was in fact nothing less than public housing itself insofar as it was being built by the city with the authorization of the state and was earmarked for a cohort of young veterans, fifteen million in number, and their spouses, who were not otherwise identified. In the first two years of Stuyvesant Town, nothing other than public agencies were involved. This was public housing on stilts.

Moses was valuable in one other respect that La Guardia was keenly aware of. With the Triborough Bridge project in the first New Deal, Moses had demonstrated that he was *shovel-ready*, 1930s slang to communicate that Moses anticipated needs and had plans and staff ready to implement solutions. Moses was a man who got things done, on his terms, of course.

Part One—The Regulatory Society

But first the federal housing law had to be settled, and as of 1935 it was in disarray. The Supreme Court had declared the housing constructed under NIRA, the National Industrial Recovery Act, to be an unconstitutional violation of the states' reserved power over housing, and so a new housing act that took into consideration the Supreme Court's ruling had first to be passed. Obviously, New York state benefited from such a ruling, and so Mayor La Guardia was content to wait. It fell to the Senator from New York to write the law, and so for a brief period everyone—a president from New York, the mayor of New York, the senator from New York, and the president of Long island's Parks Commission, the ever shovel-ready Robert Moses—were on the same page.

◆◆◆

The law, the fourth to be considered in my line up of seven laws, is also the most misunderstood, so my effort, while brief, will be to the point of achieving clarity about it. The chief purpose of the 1937 Housing Act, better known as Wagner-Steagall, was to be clear that while the Federal government might finance such housing, the states had to build it.

The first aspect to consider was that old bugaboo, *slum clearance*, as controversial a subject as any. A group generally known as the *Housers* were adamantly opposed to slum clearance as it was then conceived. Their argument was compelling: land in the city was valuable and so should not be cleared, especially since such an action would demolish existing housing for the poor. Much of such housing was sound and only needed to be renovated and better cared for.

According to Catherine Bauer, public housing should be built in the outer boroughs of the city, which in the 1930s meant Brooklyn and Queens.[6] Such land in Manhattan should be used for public purposes, like parks, universities, schools, playgrounds, and hospitals. Otherwise, such land would be snapped up by developers, who would use it to for profitable middle-class housing. Bauer's argument, and that of other housers, was compelling. If not followed, New York would put itself on a course different from that of London or Paris or any other major western city.[7] They were far from being perfect, but they had at least not made the mistake of making the city's most valuable land available to developers.[8]

The argument was sound but went against the interests of

5. Wagner-Steagall and Public Housing

demolition companies, often developers in disguise, who wanted and lobbied for the lucrative contracts for demolishing what was often the housing of their own employees. There was also the additional reason that such demolition was neatly packaged to begin with. Manhattan blocks are scribed rectangles, and so a city condemnation procedure that covered every building in the same block left the demolition company with a very nice parcel to clear. The city often kept the cleared land and built a school with its playground on it. The procedure was very convenient for everyone concerned.

The first public housing projects built under the aegis of NYCHA were built in 1937 and were the Harlem River Houses and the Williamsburg (Ten Eyck) Houses, the former with 574 units and the latter with 1,622 units. The disproportion was misleading in that it was in rough proportion to the number of African Americans and whites living in the city at the time. More than 90 percent of the residents held jobs and so were able to pay a rental fee meant to cover maintenance costs. Persons on welfare or simply too poor to afford the rent were less than 8 percent of the total residents.

Increasingly large but still low-rise public housing buildings were put up in the three remaining years before the war intervened to put a halt to public housing construction. One interesting aspect of these houses is that often they were built on land considered outside the Manhattan and thus requiring little demolition. The main examples were the Red Hook Houses with 2,545 units and the Queensbridge Houses, with over 3,000 units. Besides providing homes, these two projects provided compelling arguments that the east side of Manhattan did not have to be demolished to build adequate public housing.

The theme of this chapter is the 1937 Housing Act, better known as Wagner-Steagall, and by now enough has been said about the nuts and bolts of the legislation to be able to move on and judge its meaning.

❖❖❖

The most significant aspect of the 1937 Housing Act is not readily apparent. Where the 1934 Housing Act embodied the hope that the unskilled or deskilled working class might rise to middle class status, the 1937 Housing Act contained the admission that such social engineering might not succeed and that housing that reflected such an admission had also to be built. No such admission had been incorporated into

Part One—The Regulatory Society

the 1933 National Industrial Recovery Act. The Techwood Homes in Atlanta and the First Houses in New York City were built without any outstanding class expectations in respect to who would live there. That was no longer the case with the 1937 legislation. They were planned to house the poor. The president did in fact move in the direction of that which I am describing.

A second aspect of the 1937 Housing Act had to do with race and racism. The laws authors were Senator Robert Wagner and Congressman Henry Steagall, a northerner and a southerner. Neither man was an overt racist, but Steagall was a racial conservative, meaning that he would respect the conventions of Jim Crow as if they were time-honored traditions, which they were not. Without any particular racial animus, what fell in place was an admission that the states and not the federal government would determine the character of its housing. Even in New York State, the mandate of racial separation would be kept, but only by adhering rigorously to the Plessy rule that separate but equal was not unconstitutional. This was *Plessy v. Ferguson* at its high water mark, insofar as the equalizer of the separate facilities was best realized. The first public housing projects built, the Harlem River Houses and the Williamsburg (Ten Eyck) Houses actually did provide separate but rigorously equal facilities to the two races.

Senator Wagner was put into the position of acting as sponsor of the 1937 Housing Act. By his actions, Wagner seemed to be honoring the Jim Crow segregation, which he was not. In that respect, Wagner-Steagall was an unfortunate piece of legislation. We will have a chance to revisit it when we advance to the 1949 Housing Act, but at the moment that is far off.

A third aspect of the 1937 Housing Act is also not immediately apparent, especially in the case of African Americans. This aspect had to do with the fact that more than 90 percent of public housing units in NYCHA's jurisdiction would be rented to actively working people, a requirement that had as its by-product the guaranteed financing of public housing maintenance. For reasons that are complex, this felicitous domination by a fully employed working class would not continue after the 1960s, with the result that maintenance and the good spirits of the staff would not be maintained. This is a matter for another chapter, but at least here the positive side of emphasis on the gainfully employed working class should be mentioned.

5. Wagner-Steagall and Public Housing

Finally, the 1937 Housing Act should be put into a comparative context in which worker housing in other countries in similar situations is brought into play. Two comparison seem worth developing, the first in London with postwar "council" housing, the second in Vienna in German-Austria.

◈◈◈

In November 1918, the British government produced the Tudor Walters Report, which was heavily influenced by Raymond Unwin and the Garden Cities movement. The idea that every working-class family in Britain should live in a bucolic setting with enough outside space of lawns, trees, and clean air for a healthy life was Raymond Unwin's. That this was a middle-class concept disturbed no one. The London councils proceeded undisturbed and built the largest housing project in the world at Becontree outside London, already mentioned in an earlier footnote. The fact that Becontree had no industry, and no adequate transportation did not bother the planners. Becontree had fresh air and indoor toilets, and so everyone was happy with what they had done. London's planners had laid the basis for the creation of a commuting middle class.

In the same month that the Tudor Walters Report was published, a government led by social democrats was being formed in Vienna.[9] It too felt threatened by revolution, certainly with more justification than planners in London, and so it prioritized worker housing in Vienna. It began by commandeering buildings and socializing them, thereby gaining immediate control of existing housing. It then imposed rent-control measures and created a centralized authority for distributing apartments. Insofar as it took these actions with the approval of the Vienna populace, its actions were a demonstration of social democracy in action.

Because there were not enough existing apartments to meet demand, the Vienna council also sponsored new housing projects, the chief of which was the *Karl-Marx-Hof*, located in a Vienna suburb. That project was an integrated, low-rise building containing apartments of different sizes as well as amenities like schools, nurseries, health clinics, and laundries, all adjacent to rail transportation into the central city. Workers not accommodated in apartments in the city were eventually accommodated at the aforementioned *Karl-Marx-Hof* and at a second such project named the *George-Washington-Hof*.[10]

Part One—The Regulatory Society

Neither Britain nor German-Austria experienced working-class revolution, but clearly the Austrians had done better by the working class than their British counterparts. This is not to say that council housing in Britain did not perform the function assigned to it, namely, housing the industrial working class. It certainly did that much, but when we go beyond that basic function, problems arise. Austrian housing did not look as suburban as British housing, but by being concentrated, it managed to perform a number of other functions that made daily life easier. Perhaps the main function performed by Vienna housing was a social one. Life functions were arranged so that people would repeatedly encounter each other in contexts that were defined in social terms.

Multiple such examples could be given, but they still miss the essential point, which is that Becontree represented the wish that the working class would become middle class, while at *Karl-Marx-Hof* the working class was encouraged to be precisely what it had long been, namely, a working class with no pretensions to middle class status imposed on them by architectural design.

When we shift back to the United States, it seems clear from the home depicted in *Technical Bulletin No. 4* that the American plan for blue-collar working-class housing was dominated by middle class aspirations.[11] If that one item seems too narrow a basis for the larger argument being made, then consider every other aspect of the 1934 Housing Act. The whole notion of saving to make the 10 percent down payment requirement and then taking out a 30-year mortgage and sticking to it for the 360-month duration was entirely a middle class endeavor.

This chapter on the 1937 Housing Act is about a class of service workers who fell below the minimal threshold qualifying them for a mortgage. Correctly understood, housing planned under the legislative aegis of Wagner-Steagall was meant for those below the threshold of the industrial working class, those at work in low-paying service jobs and therefore too poor to get a mortgage.

The housing built in the remaining pre-war years before the federal government stopped funding housing built before the war was perfectly attuned to the classification of tenants described in the last sentence of the previous paragraph. My favorite of all of them is the Harlem River Houses, dated 1937 and meant for African Americans. Presumably, more than 90 percent of the families living there were headed by a

5. Wagner-Steagall and Public Housing

full-time employee. She may have been a school cafeteria worker or he a bus or taxi driver, but there was at least one real income that enabled them to pay the rent on time and help fund management to maintain the buildings and grounds.

6

Steagall-Wagner and the Creation of "Fannie Mae"

"Steagall-Wagner" looks wrong, as if the author of this book was getting things backwards, but that's not the case. It is rather the beginning of an odd but revealing story about the legislative process, one which explains why few persons can even find the so-called *1938 National Housing Act*.[1] Let me begin by offering the brief version of this unusual story.

The 1938 Housing Act, also known as "Steagall-Wagner," was nothing more than a collection of amendments to the 1937 Wagner-Steagall Act, mischievously named Steagall-Wagner to confound future law students. And the story is more complicated still, for Steagall-Wagner was also a matter of making good on promissory notes made in the 1934 Housing Act. Then finally, there is the literature, which when limited to direct consideration of the 1938 Housing Act, adds up to exactly one article that is competent and well-written.[2]

These considerations might raise the question why anyone would bother with such a complicated law and why as well the 1938 Housing Act is one of the seven laws that this book addresses. The reason is simple: the collection of amendments that make up the 1938 Housing Act are the foundation stones of the Federal National Mortgage Association (FNMA), better known as Fannie Mae. By the 1960s, the confusing Fannie Mae was managing a trillion dollars' worth of American home mortgages. Developments beyond its first fifteen years will not concern us in this book, and even the first fifteen years will not concern us as much as will the original idea and concept of Fannie Mae.

❖❖❖

6. Steagall-Wagner and the Creation of "Fannie Mae"

As it should be, the original idea for Fannie Mae was relatively simple. Mortgages granted by savings and loans generated interest that was lower than market rates but higher than that earned by savings accounts. Hence, such mortgages fitted nicely into the hopes and fears of a large category of small investors who wanted to have their money earn more than was offered for savings accounts but were shy about getting into the stock market. Conventionally, such people invested in bonds or for the riskier ones, index funds or mutuals. Most such people would also be happy with mortgages, if they could get them, and in the form of mortgage-backed securities or collateralized debt-obligations, there was no good reason they could not get them. These were people who were not interested in gambling but only wanted a secure old age.

The notion of "little old ladies" buying such securities is also misleading. Across the land, there were any number of institutional investors who were conservative in their tastes. Teachers unions or for that matter pension funds. Many of them tailored their investment strategies to individuals by asking them how much risk they wanted to shoulder through their retirement accounts. Even banks and savings institutions that wanted to have their reserves bear money without running significant risks were interested. Any number of institutional investors would be inclined to invest risk-averse funds in the kind of packages the Federal National Mortgage Association had to offer.

The amendments imposed on the 1937 Housing Act in January 1938 added up to 19 pages single-spaced, making the 1938 Housing Act nearly as long as its predecessor. Understanding it was a challenge but one that was simplified by J.W. Brabner-Smith in the article he wrote for the *American Bar Association Journal*, previously mentioned and footnoted.

At its outset, the Federal National Mortgage Association (FNMA) was a small operation funded adequately and staffed by persons capable of making a commonsense sales pitch to presidents of S&Ls. The argument was simple: debt is a fluid process that fuels worry and stimulates efforts to eliminate it, a good analogy being the way one seeks to eliminate a mosquito bite by scratching it. It doesn't go away. It just itches all the more.

Debt can be structured to the creditor's advantage, as it is by moneylenders in the countryside of India. They lend money and demand only that the interest be paid. They collect on schedule and send thugs to put muscle into their insistence. If the monsoons are good, there are few problems. If the monsoon fails, as it invariable does every few years, the farmer just goes deeper into debt and has to work that much harder to pay the interest. American home loans in the 1920s were similar, which was why Winfield Riefler complained so often about them.

Well-structured debt is a commodity that can be sold, if packaged appropriately, in which respect the idea of the mortgage was one of the best packaging schemes seen in a long time. A man signing on the dotted line was incurring a commitment to make payments over 360 consecutive months, or thirty years. He would not have to be chased by thugs at the end of each month. Instead, he or his wife would come to the lender and happily pay the debt, convinced that it was a species of savings. The books would be kept not by the moneylender making a notation in a grubby book but by the local bank in a clean set of books kept in a safe. Finally, the debt was insured by the federal government. Nothing could possibly go wrong.

The government was now offering to sell such debt in the form of securities, or units that would go to the highest bidder in periodic auctions. Furthermore, the units could be resold by the holder for any reason, no questions asked. So if the holder's daughter was getting married and he suddenly needed a great deal of cash, then for a small price the agent he had engaged had one to sell.

Winfield Riefler knew all of this when he presided over the creation of the 1934 Housing Act, the nation's first such legislation. The explanations that he forgot, that he was negligent, that he had no time to so act, don't hold up.[3] The actual reason is simple and was at the time compelling: the 1934 Housing Act was passed but local banks owned no mortgages, and so there were none to package and sell. It was as simple as that.

By 1937 or early 1938, it was abundantly clear that local banks had negotiated a sufficient number of loans to justify passage of the legislation omitted in 1934. At that point, something called *mortgage-backed securities* (MBS) could be created. Even if we lacked statistics, solely the creation of Fannie Mae would tell us that the 1934 Housing Act had by late-1937 or early 1938 been deemed a success.

◈◈◈

In January of 1938 when the amendments comprising the 1938 Housing Act were passed as a package, the New Deal was drawing to a

6. Steagall-Wagner and the Creation of "Fannie Mae"

close and a new era was beginning. Just three months earlier, on October 5, 1937, and in Chicago, the president had put up a trial balloon in a speech called "Quarantine the Aggressor." It was sharply criticized by the editorial board of the *Chicago Tribune*, and so Roosevelt retreated. But his retreat was mainly tactical. Roosevelt henceforth decided to move quietly and incrementally toward taking a stand against Nazi Germany and fascist Italy. He would do so by becoming a supplier of equipment and arms to Britain. Month by month, Roosevelt's mind was increasingly taken up with this aspect of presidential policy. The New Deal was being left behind by the man in the Oval Office because greater problems had arisen.

With the Quarantine the Aggressor speech and the creation of Fannie Mae, we are thus at a crossroads in the progression of this book, one in which it is appropriate to ask some basic questions. The most basic of which has to do with the consumer society. Had it in any sense of the term been created? The most likely answer is that the consumer society in which this book is most interested was a post-war phenomenon and so the many legislative acts we have surveyed to this point, five in total, are previews of coming attractions. This answer would be completely satisfactory if it were not for the act that we have reviewed in this chapter, for the agency it created, Fannie Mae, was as good an indicator as one might ask for that the 1934 Housing Act was a success. Americans in sufficient numbers understood the 1934 law not just in a passive sense but well enough to commit to purchasing a home being built somewhere. Yet there is more to the story than just this.

The national economy had begun to recover from the depths of 1933 with the result that everything had become less than dire, giving Roosevelt more elbow room than he might have expected at any time in his first term. In all likelihood, this meant that the administration had decided to treat the emerging blue-collar working class as a potential addition to the middle class by defining their housing and financial arrangements in updated middle-class terms. That issue—how to define the blue-collar working class—had moved a long way toward resolution between 1934 and 1938. It was clear from the 1937 strike in Flint, Michigan, that unskilled assembly line workers were entering the mainstream, a trend that was even clearer a year later.

In 1938, much of this success was assigned to 1935 Wagner Act, and so with the passage of an additional two pieces of legislation in 1937 and

Part One—The Regulatory Society

1938, all of which had his name on them, Senator Robert Wagner of New York had emerged as one of the continuing New Deal's most significant players. Among his achievements, hardly noticed even at the time, was that the 1937 Wagner-Steagall Act had successfully put a floor under the working class housing anticipated in the 1934 Housing Act by providing differently for a third segment of the working class: those unable to afford even a mortgaged house.

The suddenly articulating working class might now be said to have three classifications: the skilled working class being serviced by the 1933 Home Owner's Loan Act; the unskilled blue-collar working class of Detroit's assembly lines, now being serviced by the 1934 Housing Act, and the service workers being provided for by the 1937 Housing Act. There was as well the 1938 Housing Act that created the financing for much of the housing being built. Suddenly, if it were not for the gathering storm of war, the United States was articulating the internal structures of a working-class society. Suddenly everything had been put in place for the machinery of the private sector and government to start meshing with each other in a huge spending machine.

But all the while a *force majeure* of a different sort had been intruding. Hitler occupied the Rhineland, and Mussolini invaded what was then called Abyssinia. The president dropped everything, to use the common way of putting such matters, to give his undivided attention to world politics. Even as early as two years before the outbreak of hostilities, the United States was becoming the "arsenal of democracy," to use the phrase that would grow in popularity because it described the U.S. role with uncanny accuracy. The consumer society was put on hold to make room for war, a war in which the United States would be the allied supply-chain. But already before the war outlines of the post-war consumer society was visible.

There was no real necessity for wartime austerity. On the contrary, the United States was quite capable of producing butter as well as guns. It need only have built new facilities, and judged by Ford's River Rouge complex, it knew how to do that as well. Perhaps producing automobiles and homes would have been pushing matters too far, but everything short of those two items could have been easily produced.

Instead, the next seven years on the domestic front were dominated by a policy of exaggerated austerity. The more war took center stage, the fewer consumer items there were to purchase. Automobile production

6. Steagall-Wagner and the Creation of "Fannie Mae"

ceased from 1942 to 1945. in their place, non-market items like bombers and tanks were produced, and food was rationed. The blue-collar work force was opened to women, with males donning khaki and heading overseas.

World War II was for the United States a reprise of World War I. In the earlier conflict, the United States was also the arsenal of democracy, specifically British and French democracy. The later conflict was more complicated, but it was clear from the "bases-for-destroyers deal" that Britain could not have held out even through 1940 without being propped up by the United States.[4]

By the time the United States eased into the post-war in the summer of 1945, everyone was too busy celebrating victory to ask how much of it had been a theater that might have been disregarded. Of course, the answer was that theatricality was integral to the war effort and so could not have been avoided. Nonetheless, the creation of the conditions of consumer society so soon after the end of the conflict should have raised a question about the character of the American involvement. It didn't, even from the dour Stalin, who didn't have too many illusions about the war.

The arsenal of the democracy phenomenon started up again in 1947, less than two years after the end of the hot war, this time heralding the onset of Cold War with Stalin's Soviet Union. How except in the way it was clothed did the Marshall Plan differ from the United States being the chief supplier of Germany's enemies in both world wars? However one answers that question, by June 5, 1947, when George Marshall announced his plan, the consumer society had started. It began with the first model year of genuinely postwar automobiles. It was also coughing and wheezing its way into existence in a New York suburb called "Desert Palms," which would soon be renamed *Levittown*.

❖❖❖

Like one of those Four Minute Men of the previous World War, I would snatch this opportunity to renew an argument integral to this book, which is that the consumer society was not the intention of any single person or law. It was rather the product of multiple laws laying the groundwork for a society in which ordinary Americans, most of whom still Grant Wood types in the 1930s, would mutate into prolific spenders. The key element was not the car but rather the home, and while its rough outlines were laid out in multiple pieces of 1930s legislation, it was nowhere more clearly sketched than in the 1934 Housing Act and in the FHA's *Technical Bulletin No. 4*. Everything was also anticipated in Ford's Sociological Department, but that entire operation was premature. The New Deal spelled out much of that vision of the American Dream in more practical terms.

7

The 1945 Amended GI Bill and American Racism

On the day the GI Bill was passed and became law, American troops were still in Normandy not more than 25 miles from the beaches where they had landed.[1] The Germans would fight a final Normandy action at Falaise, but once they had lost that battle, they were compelled to retreat to a much wider front. It was only a matter of months before the war in Europe would be over and won.

There is no point in being coy about the terms of the 1944 legislation, the sixth act leading up to the consumer society. It promised discounted educational benefits, but these excited few GIs in Normandy in the spring of 1944. If their eyes were not on the retreating Germans, they were on the prospect of Paris and celebrations of victory in that storied city. It is doubtful if any GI gave any thought to his "readjustment" in the postwar back home.

In fact, the GI Bill would not be meaningful to this book until it was amended in September 1945 to eliminate the down payment requirement on the purchase of homes under terms virtually identical to those of the 1934 Housing Act. It is difficult to know today if the authors of the 1945 amendment understood how significant their amendment was. With the advantage of some hindsight, we today are in a vastly better position to grasp its significance. The men in uniform in the final months of the war were ordinary Americans with little savings and without much money in their pockets. A ten percent down payment on a home that sold for $7,500 would have cost them an immediate $750 in cash. Very few men had that much cash on hand, and so the down payment requirement was a formidable barrier to taking advantage of the GI Bill.

At the time the amendment was added to the GI Bill, a building

Part One—The Regulatory Society

contractor named Bill Levitt was thinking about the small potato farms of eastern Nassau County on Long Island. More than 70,000 acres of Long Island's sandy land was dedicated to such farming. Poor farmland, it nonetheless had excellent drainage and was easy to build on. Levitt had spent the war constructing barrack buildings on slabs of poured concrete, putting 2×4s, plywood, sheetrock, shingle-roofing, and millwork windows into two-story buildings with outside staircases and entrances. But that was Bill Levitt's past. When spring 1946 came, Levitt was solely concerned with negotiating preliminary agreements with the county's many potato farmers.

When Levitt began construction in 1947, his place was named Island Trees and the few finished homes were for rent to interested parties, mainly from nearby Brooklyn. At the time, working class families were leaving Brooklyn for the borough of Queens and Levitt thought he could pick up an overflow because his homes had more charm than those being built by developers in Queens.

The difference was immediately obvious. New York City was filled with start-up contractors with little money. They purchased single lots and put up attached buildings to maximize the space they had bought. In sum, they did not deviate a bit from the builders of brownstones a half-century earlier, except that the results were uglier. In the suburbs, Levitt could draw a wider lot and put a more attractive and *detached* home on it, a feature that was of decisive importance in the eyes of the beholder.

Without the down payment requirement, the monthly cost of buying a home was not much more than the cost of renting one. Apparently, Levitt had not thought of this, although it is hard to believe that so clever a man would allow such a thought to slip past him. Nonetheless, legend has it that visitors to Island Trees repeatedly told Levitt they would prefer purchasing to renting one of his homes. One fine day the electric light bulb went off above Levitt's head and he got the idea.

Levitt changed the name of Island Trees to Levittown, put his homes up for sale, and to the persistent question whether he would have a Stuyvesant Town moment in which African American veterans tried to buy homes, Levitt responded that his project would remain racially harmonious, meaning completely white. At first, he put this in writing, but with *Shelley v. Kraemer* decided by the Supreme Court in 1948, the guarantee was downgraded to verbal status.[2] By 1949 the sputtering,

7. The 1945 Amended GI Bill and American Racism

coughing two-stroke motor of the Island Trees venture was becoming a sleek modern engine of profit called *Levittown*.

The reaction was not slow in coming. For three years, Levitt's homes sold before they were finished, with white working-class Brooklynites often buying after simply seeing the location on a map or in a muddy field. By 1951, when the original Levittown was completed, 17,441 homes had been built and sold.[3]

◈◈◈

The background to this chapter has to do with the legislative arrangements made to compensate American servicemen who had fought in World War I. That's the First, not the Second, World War. Initially, there was not only no compensation but also the claim, repeated by Republican politicians many times, that true patriots sought no "bonus" for having done one's duty for one's country. The Veterans of Foreign Wars and the newly founded American Legion based their existence on lobbying for such benefits but were not supported by the Republican Party of Warren Harding.

Nonetheless, the VFW and the Legion kept the issue alive and were sustained in their efforts by examples both negative and positive of overseas veterans' organizations, although not always in the way expected. In Germany, the *Stahlhelm* was a powerful counterpart to the American Legion. It demonstrated to anyone willing to look closely the difficulty of readjustment to a "civil" life after a war. The situation was not nearly so dire for British veterans, but this was due to a strong commitment on the part of postwar governments to build "Homes Fit for Heroes" to which veterans of the trenches at Ypres and the Somme were given priority.

Every British government made good on that commitment, giving Britain its first wave of what came to be called "council housing." The oddest thing about council housing was its typical location outside rather than inside cities, noted in an earlier chapter on the Becontree estate located outside London. It was a massive project, fully replicated by a similar one near Manchester. Midlands cities followed similar patterns, locating such housing on defunct estates that had been abandoned outside manufacturing cities. All of these estates, using the latter term in a second sense as "council estates," were ways of warehousing the earlier working class with housing that was attractive but distant from factories. It forced residents who had jobs to spend a

Part One—The Regulatory Society

great deal of time commuting and made life especially difficult for factory workers.

I mention and emphasize the location of the Becontree estate because it played some small part in the American decision to locate suburban housing "estates" like Island Trees in locations outside cities. The connection is weak, however, and should not be emphasized. The main reason for the location of the American suburbs was the low cost of garden farmland.

Harding passed away in 1923 to be succeeded by Calvin Coolidge, who was equally opposed to paying the veterans a bonus. While vetoing a bill to provide funds, Coolidge expressed the sentiment that, "patriotism which is bought and paid for is not patriotism." Under pressure, Congress then overrode his veto and on May 19, 1924, passed the World War Adjusted Compensation Act, which granted veterans certificates allowing them future payments that became valid in 1945.[4]

A feature of the legislation provided that after 1927 such payments could be used as collateral to secure loans.[5] By June 30, 1932, more than 2.5 million veterans had borrowed $1, 369 billion.[6] There are two ways to understand such borrowing. The first is that veterans wanted cash immediately and borrowing against their certificates as collateral was a backdoor way of getting it. They thus hurried to a local bank, took out a loan on the basis of their Adjusted Compensation Act certificate, defaulted on the loan, and let the bank redeem the note with the federal government. This way of getting the promised compensation is unlikely to have been used. In any case, there is little or no evidence from the banks that then existed.

The second and more likely use of certificates of the Adjusted Compensation Act is that veterans borrowed money to purchase homes. Assuming the certificates had an average worth of about $500, such certificates might enable veterans to borrow enough to make the down payment on a home costing $5,000.[7] How much of this was done is difficult to ascertain, but what is significant for this book is that the idea of doing so was at work. It might reasonably have been assumed by the authors of the 1933 Home Owners' Loan Act and might also have been a consideration in the making of the 1934 Housing Act. These are speculations, however, and so nothing rests upon them.

The 1924 legislation was hardly the end of trouble for the federal

7. The 1945 Amended GI Bill and American Racism

government. Depression compounded the problems of some veterans by rendering many among them unemployed. Thousands of such veterans descended on the nation's capital to stage an unheard-of protest, a sit-in, or in their case, a camp-in on the mall. The president ordered the police to evict them, and when the police needed help, Hoover ordered Gen. Douglas MacArthur to deal with the veterans. He brought in troops backed up by five tanks.[8]

To be sure, the so-called "Bonus Army" was routed from the mall, but the experience created an image that would long last as a memory. Men having to camp out because they had lost their homes were living in "Hoovervilles." Men sleeping on park benches covered themselves with "Hoover Blankets," or what was left of that day's newspaper. The president who had called in Douglas MacArthur had arguably done a respectable job in dealing with the depression, but all that went down the drain when he was tarred with the way he had handled the veterans' protest.

Roosevelt would prove to be no more sympathetic to the veterans than Hoover was, but at least he knew how to get out of the way when political harm threatened to get into the way. An Adjusted Compensation Payment Act was passed, vetoed by President Roosevelt, with Congress then overriding the president's veto.[9] Contrary to the reputation for being a spendthrift bestowed on him by Republican critics, President Roosevelt was a fiscal conservative and would remain one all his life. He said as much in his first Inaugural Address, affirmed it by vetoing the Adjusted Compensation Payment Act, and would affirm his fiscal conservatism again when the time came to produce a bonus act for the veterans of World War II.

◆◆◆

For the argument of this book, the amended G.I Bill is more significant than the original law. According to its provisions, no down payment was required and any loan on real estate up to a maximum of $4,000 would be guaranteed by the government (as compared with a $2,000 limit under the1944 law). It was expected that such loans would then be amortized over a period up to twenty-five years. Any lending agency which was subject to examination and supervision by federal and state government agencies was authorized to make the loans, and the loan became automatically guaranteed as soon as the lending agency and the veteran sign the final agreement.[10]

Part One—The Regulatory Society

The provisions described above were at the heart of the consumer society to come, so the reader might reasonably ask why the author of this book did not just begin it with the 1945 amended GI Bill. The answer is that the loan provisions of the GI Bill were modeled on the 1934 Housing Act, which had been fleshed out by the 1938 Housing Act creating Fannie Mae. In turn, the 1934 Housing Act would not have been conceived in the absence of the model provided by the 1933 Home Owner's Loan Act, and none of this would have happened without the shield provided savings & loan banks by the 1933 Banking Act, or Glass-Steagall.

The words of the previous paragraph provide a rigid model of action. In fact, everything was more flexible and fluid than I am indicating. The legislation of the 1930s allowed a social mind-set to emerge and develop. In place of widespread distrust, the various pieces of legislation created trust in the government. The Wall Street banks were prevented from corrupting the Main Street financial institutions, and furthermore the latter held deposits that were guaranteed by *their* government, which for once was not trying to pit them against each other. None of this was due to the good will of any individual law makers. It was rather the product of the unintended working of several laws passed in response to their own difficulties.

Such reasoning included the chief sponsor of the 1944 Servicemen's Readjustment Act: Republican Congresswoman Edith Nourse Rogers of Massachusetts. The actual author of the legislation was Harry W. Colmery, then head of the American Legion and also a former member of the Republican national committee. The legislation endured in its original form until 1956, when it was replaced by new legislation. In keeping with his fiscal conservatism, President Roosevelt was not in favor of the bill as originally written. He favored making grants or loans only to veterans who qualified on economic grounds, which is to say, to economically impoverished veterans.

The surprising aspect of these notations was that no sponsor or author was a southerner, an uncharacteristic omission that was quickly corrected when Mississippi Congressman John E. Rankin joined Congresswoman Nourse Rogers to sponsor the bill. Nourse Rogers was the first chairperson of the House Committee on Veterans Affairs, created by the Legislative Reorganization Act of 1946.[11] She was succeeded by Rankin when Republicans won control of the House in the 1946 mid-term elections but returned to the

7. The 1945 Amended GI Bill and American Racism

position when the Democratic Party regained control of the House in the 1948 election.

Lest one conclude that Rankin joined Nourse in order to save the soul of his party, one would be advised to think again. In the ordering of racists prevalent at the time, Rankin stood alone. So virulent was his racism that he was inclined to disturb the decorum of he House by using the N word in his speeches, a practice he then defended by claiming that his listeners had been deceived by the way Rankin pronounced "Negro."

The amended GI Bill (to use its popular name) has gained its greatest fame from its educational programs, but from the outset such programs were mired in more controversy than is usually admitted.[12] Such wrangling was not specific to the GI Bill but was often a consequence of an imbalance between expenditures and controls. The GI Bill promised the expenditure of vast amounts of money but with questionable controls, mainly because the program would be administered not by the federal government but rather by the states.[13] A number of existing or potential educational institutions saw opportunity and began looking into mounting educational programs for veterans.

In 1945 the immediate problem in respect to the GI Bill had to do with historic black colleges and universities (HBCU). At the time, Southern states practiced discrimination by law and so had lawful reason to redirect African American veterans to HBCU. But then they also had reason to distribute funding in proportion to the number of students being so redirected, a procedural mandate that was not always honored. As a consequence, HBCU were not able to manage the number of additional students imposed on them. The overall result was that African American veterans were systematically denied the opportunity for higher education.

In contrast, a disproportionate amount of federal funding was available to segregated white universities, like the flagship state universities in every Southern state. While they had little problem dealing with the increase of students, there was a problem with the increase as a whole, for many of the white student applicants were not qualified for the rigors of higher education. Consequently, there arose more questionable institutions willing to take less qualified students. Some failed quickly, but what were the state governments to do about the flow of veterans who were not adequately qualified?[14] The easy solution was to

Part One—The Regulatory Society

certify the programs of the new institutions, a process that was conventionally placed in the hands of outside agencies but was now bypassed or handled by state agencies.

Similar problems did not exist with the program to support home ownership. In most respects, it was self-enforcing, as a veteran qualified for a government guaranteed home mortgage was not going to want to squander his one opportunity to be a homeowner. The program was administered under the aegis of state law, and southern state law in the 1940s mandated segregation in housing. Hence, African American veterans eligible for GI Bill housing benefits could not easily find housing that qualified. When they did, it was in an African American neighborhood, which more than likely meant that it was red lined and so disqualified for that reason. The overall result was that African American veterans were boxed out of the GI Bill housing benefits. Finally, to make matters even more difficult for African American veterans, they were told that they were questionable as veterans because they had not really fought in the war. The reason of course was that they had been segregated in the military, being put in their own units and made to mostly perform service jobs. They could not have fought even if they had wanted to.

◈◈◈

As World War I demonstrated, veterans afflicted with a great deal of combat experience are a difficult lot. They seldom adjust easily to civilian life in the postwar. In his novel, *All Quiet on the Western Front*, Erich Maria Remarque has his hero Paul Bäumer say how difficult if not impossible it will be to readjust to civil life after years at the front. Remarque was correct in his appraisal of the problem, for the more front experience a soldier had, the more difficult he found readjustment to civilian conditions after the war. When members of Congress named the GI Bill the *Servicemen's Readjustment Act*, they correctly identified the chief problem of the postwar for these men and women. It would be *readjustment* to civilian life.

At the end of World War II, there were more than fifteen million American veterans, about fourteen million of whom were white and so likely to get the benefits promised in the GI Bill. For the most part, they had no money, but many of them would quickly marry women who did have money from having worked in defense industries during the war. Those women were quickly dismissed from their jobs to make way for

7. The 1945 Amended GI Bill and American Racism

returning veterans, and so a situation was created where fully employed young men were being attached to young women with bursting bank accounts and aspirations to produce children. The stage was set for a new kind of society. Only one additional law was needed, and it was already in the pipe.

8

African American Exodus and the 1949 Housing Act

The title listed above embraces different kinds of material, but here both are included in one and the same chapter, a matter of efficiency. There are further internal divisions, such as two separate migrations out of the south and several different bills adding up to the 1949 legislation, but they will not delay the narrative to follow.

For the quarter century before World War I broke out, social relations in the South were dominated by two events of significance. The first was the 1895 Atlanta Compromise worked out by the Tuskegee educator Booker T. Washington and a collection of white leaders.[1] By that agreement, African Americans would accept their subordinate position in return for adequately funded educational facilities and a guarantee of justice in the law. The fact that Booker T. Washington had even to seek such guarantees was a sure indicator that they were not to be found in the South of the time.

The second event came a year later and was the Supreme Court decision in *Plessy v. Ferguson* to the effect that separate but equal facilities were not unconstitutional.[2] The key element of *Plessy* was not so much the decision itself as the dissent of John M. Harlan. In his opinion, Harlan argued that in the social reality of the South, facilities that were separate would most decidedly *not* be equal. On the contrary, the norm *separate but equal* would be inverted to read separate but unequal, which would make them involuntary and segregated. In hindsight, it was this inversion that made the Atlanta Compromise interesting.

The real issue, of course, was not with railroad cars but rather with schooling. The education of children, but not the public character of their schools, had become a mandate after the Civil War. The problem

8. African American Exodus and the 1949 Housing Act

for southern white supremacists was how to satisfy the mandate to educate all children while making sure that African American children received a poor education. The preferred way of doing so was to keep African American schools systematically underfunded and so understaffed or poorly staffed. That much was deemed enough to keep the next generation of African Americans in ignorance and so socially inferior. It was this confluence of problems that Booker T. Washington was trying to head off with the Atlanta Compromise.[3]

The other great opponent of the Jim Crow character of the era was W.E.B. Du Bois, whose outstanding distinction was to be the recipient of the best education money could buy. He had been a student at the University of Berlin at a time when it was the leading university of the world, and he had returned to the United States to earn a doctorate at Harvard University which then as now was America's leading institution. Du Bois led the "Talented Tenth," a group of similarly inclined African Americans who opposed the Atlanta Compromise by insisting that African Americans mount a protest movement that demanded equality without conditions. Du Bois went on to become one of the founding members of the National Association for the Advancement of Colored People, or NAACP in 1909 and worked to impose his agenda on it.

Du Bois stated his objections to Booker T. Washington's Atlanta Compromise in his book, *The Souls of Black Folk*.[4] Du Bois's most basic objection was to the kind of social unity aspired to by Washington. For Du Bois, there was no escaping a *double consciousness* in African Americans that reflected an unresolvable social divide. At all times African Americans had to be aware of how they viewed themselves and how they were viewed by others, namely, members of the predominantly white society. Du Bois's double consciousness is a species of what later came to be called "Queer" consciousness, and it gave to African Americans an entirely different perspective on the world. Du Bois wanted African Americans to become normal persons.

Perhaps more significant for Du Bois was another aspect of social consciousness, that of the triangular character of the white mind in the historic South. The world of the white imagination was made up of black men, white women, and white men. Since the aftermath of the Civil War, African American men had been depicted as predators and rapists. The social function of white men, organized for the purpose, was to protect white women from black men, which is to say, from rapists. This theme emerged after the Civil War, led to the organization of

Part One—The Regulatory Society

the original Ku Klux Klan, and was depicted in D.W. Griffith's 1915 film, *Birth of a Nation*. The film was made on the basis of a script by a graduate school friend of Woodrow Wilson's. The friendship endured, and when the former New Jersey governor became president, the film was given a premiere showing in the White House. To this day, that event serves as prima facie evidence of Wilson's racism.[5]

I am emphasizing the sexual depiction of African American men as rapists because that slander was basic to much that transpired at the social and political levels of southern and later American society.[6] A film like *Birth of a Nation* put the slander into the form of a libel and so contributed to the revival of the Klan in the 1920s in states outside the South, like Indiana.

More subtly, the slander or libel crept into the legal system in the form of ordinances meant to be enforced by local residents if not by the authorities. They could be temporal, spatial, or both. Temporal ordinances took the form of "sundown" regulations, which allowed in African American handymen and cleaning women during sunlit hours but demanded they be out of town by sundown. Spatial ordinances took the form of so-called zoning regulations, which prohibited members of a one race from living in a neighborhood where the majority of residents were from a different race.

❖❖❖

One such set of zoning regulations was passed by the city of Louisville, Kentucky. The ordinance, or regulation, held that a person could not buy or build a home in a neighborhood where the majority of residents were of a different race. All such zoning ordinances contrived to look even-handed: a black man could not buy in a majority white neighborhood, and a white man could not buy in a majority black neighborhood. Not surprisingly, suspicion was rife that the ordinance was aimed at African Americans.

What came next was genuinely surprising, however. William Warley, a black lawyer, purchased a building lot from Charles H. Buchanan, a white man, and conditioned his purchase on his being able to live in the home that he would build. Warley then refused to honor his contract because a Louisville ordinance made it impossible to live in what he built.

Buchanan, the white plaintiff, then sued Warley for failure to complete the contract, arguing that the Louisville ordinance was an illegal

8. African American Exodus and the 1949 Housing Act

impediment to a legitimate contract. Both sides had managed to get on the side of the angels by arguing the dignity of contract, a central element of the American concept of a commercial society.[7]

The case was a brilliant staging of the issue of racism in American housing, with the parties reversing roles in counter-intuitive fashion. Justice Oliver Wendell Holmes recognized the ruse and declared the case to be "manufactured" by the parties. But then Holmes reversed himself and joined the majority by agreeing with Buchanan that the ordinance was illegal. The clever Warley, evidently a follower of W.E.B. Du Bois, had lost the case but affirmed a principle important to his employer at the time, which perhaps not coincidentally was the NAACP.[8]

The effect of zoning regulations like the one contested in *Buchanan v. Warley* was to open the way to other maneuvers that were not illegal but nonetheless had the effect of excluding African Americans. For example, a municipality might pass a restriction mandating it to be illegal for more than one family to live in a home in the municipality. If sued, the city's lawyers could argue that the restriction was not aimed at African Americans, who tended to double up because they were poor, but was rather intended to maintain property values. If plaintiff had to prove malign intention, then plaintiff would lose because there was none, at least none that could be shown.

In the above manner, what gradually arose in the 1920s were the first versions of color-coded maps that ranked neighborhoods according to their credit-worthiness. The least credit worthy section of a municipality would be the one in which existing homes were oldest and most in need of renovation. These would be ineligible for mortgages. But since African Americans were the poorest people, the identified neighborhood would also be the one where African Americans happened to live, and so the bans were effectively denying mortgages to African Americans but without the perceivable intention of doing so.

By the time the 1934 Housing Act was passed, savings-and-loan institutions were producing and using maps that were color-coded according to credit worthiness. Without showing any malign intentions, the maps included a typical red zone with a warning to banks that homes in that area were bad investments. That the area zoned red or to use the favored term, *red lined*, happened to be occupied by African Americans was irrelevant to the argument of the involved savings and loans.

Part One—The Regulatory Society

If by this point the reader's head is spinning, think how confusing it was in the first New Deal when a supposedly liberal Roosevelt administration was guaranteeing mortgage loans delivered through local Main Street banks. Such institutions were committed by tradition and regulatory law to make the best use of their clients' savings when making loans. Without ever saying as much, the 1934 Housing Act was unlikely to finance any construction taking place in an area that was red-lined.

And so the Roosevelt administration, without any overtly racist intention, began to involve itself in programs that were institutionally racist. Such programs could not be identified by intentions but only by its effects, but this alone was not enough to support litigation. Courts were accustomed to giving close scrutiny to malign intentionality, and where there was none, then the program could not be found to be racist, regardless of effect, even when that was racially biased.

The South since the Civil War had tended to be a one-party monopoly, with the result that Democrats elected to Congress accumulated more seniority than their Northern counterparts and so held all the chairmanships when the Democratic Party was in the majority. This meant that committee chairmen tended to author legislation or minimally have a veto over its content. When it became clear that the Roosevelt administration was intent on legislating programs that would benefit a growing class of factory workers, Southern legislators had no objection as long as the legislation explicitly excluded agricultural workers and domestic servants, south or north. Hence, the beneficiaries might be steel workers from Birmingham in Alabama or from Pittsburgh, Pennsylvania, but they could not be farm workers in North Dakota or Mississippi.

The exclusion of domestic help from every piece of New Deal legislation signed into law by President Roosevelt was an even clearer indication that the law in question intended a racist effect. Of course, the law applied to white as well as black women, but since there were virtually no white maids or kitchen help in the South, the excluded category happened to be nearly entirely African American women.

And so the reaction that began with *Buchanan v. Warley* metastasized into a widespread program of institutional racism over the course of the New Deal/Fair Deal period we are covering.

◈ ◈ ◈

8. *African American Exodus and the 1949 Housing Act*

Through most of the period described above, change in the American South was also happening on an entirely different dimension, one that might best be thought of as wholesale as opposed to retail. African Americans were beginning to leave the South for the North in numbers large enough to make the movement worthy of attention in its own right. To be sure, African Americans had fled the South even before the Civil War and made their way along the underground railroad to sanctuaries in the North or even as far away as Canada. Some had left after the Civil War in response to Klan violence. But beginning in the middle of the second decade of the 20th century, a movement began that was entirely different.[9]

The cause, at least the direct cause, of the new movement was economic rather than racial. With the onset of world war in Europe, a vast wave of prosperity hit the manufacturing North as the consequence of contracts negotiated with the allies, Britain and France. Most if not all of this money was concentrated in the Upper Midwest, or in the states of Pennsylvania, Ohio, Michigan, Indiana, Wisconsin, and Illinois. The money meant that jobs were available, perhaps not the highest paying jobs, but even service jobs of sweeping floors and cleaning machines paid better than the farm jobs in the South.

Though African Americans were spread across the South, they were funneled to the North over two routes. The first was up the Mississippi River to any number of destinations but usually Chicago. Along the way, African Americans might already have relatives in Memphis or St. Louis and disembark there, or they might go on to Minneapolis, Milwaukee, or Detroit, but if they did, Chicago was still a pivot point on the journey.

Alternatively, African Americans headed by the same means of transportation up the early version of I-95 in the direction of New York City, some meeting relatives in Baltimore or Philadelphia. From New York City, some changed busses and headed on to Boston or Cleveland.

The migration of African Americans described above tapered off after the World War I, leaving a vibrant jazz scene in Chicago's south side, a cultural renaissance in Harlem in New York, and the faint beginnings of a music scene in the Motor City of Detroit, later nicknamed "Motown." These beachheads then came alive again with the beginning of World War II and the onset of a larger African American migration northwards.

The outstanding characteristic of the latter migration was that it did not stop when the war came to an end. On the contrary, it increased

Part One—The Regulatory Society

in density, still primarily by means of Greyhound buses. The first questions in respect to this second migration had to do with how large it was and whether anyone was noticing. No one knew the answer to those questions or how long the migration would go on. Not many persons knew about a phenomenon that still had no name, but political leaders of both parties were aware and were reminded again and again by metaphorical description or sheer brute fact that an immense social change was occurring.

In a number of unrelated incidents, change began to come to the American racial scene. In 1944, for instance, a Swedish scholar published a book called *An American Dilemma*, where he made a case for the integration of public schools.[10] In baseball one year later, Jackie Robinson was recruited by the Brooklyn Dodgers to begin the integration of professional sports. In national politics, President Truman integrated the armed forces of the United States. By 1948, a young politician from Minnesota named Hubert Horatio Humphrey succeeded in placing a plank in the party platform that committed the party to oppose racial segregation. Senator Strom Thurmond of South Carolina led a third party, imaginatively named *Dixiecrats*, to combat such change. All along the way, the NAACP sponsored cases designed to test the judicial waters and give Fred Vinson's Supreme Court the opportunity to respond with legal mandates.

Sooner or later such turmoil had to reach into the field of housing. As we saw in the previous chapter, the 1945 amended GI Bill offered white veterans, of which there were more than thirteen million, low-interest loans with the down payment waived for the purchase of homes. Southern Congressional leaders, ever resourceful, managed to have the entire program implemented by state agencies, or rather agencies that were bound by state law, ensuring that most if not all of the loans went to white veterans and as few as possible to African American veterans.

In the agrarian South, there was no visible housing problem, for collections of field hands could always be housed on the back fields, away from the main roads, in whatever shanties could be built there. But in the manufacturing North, the tendency of African Americans was to congregate in the poorest sections of cities, where the rents were lowest, and there to overload already run-down apartments with too many inhabitants. Social life spilled out onto the street, with black men congregating at street corners to get away from the women and children

8. African American Exodus and the 1949 Housing Act

back in the tenements.[11] The men sought work in the mills and factories, the women as domestics by gathering at their own appointed spots to constitute an instant labor market for cleaning women.

For the most enterprising of African American men, an intolerable situation was addressed by seeking to rent or buy housing elsewhere in the cities, as for example at Detroit's *Eight Mile Wall*, where whites had responded to African Americans seeking to purchase property by building a cement wall of separation.[12] Whereas segregation took on a soft look in the South, it tended to take on the hardest of edges in Northern cities, often in the form of regulations that allowed no exceptions.

◆◆◆

It was in this context that legislators in the 79th Congress were more or less pressured to legislate in response to the growing housing crisis facing African Americans. From its outset in 1946, the legislation had three sponsors, a Democrat, a Republican, and a reliable Southern Democrat to ensure that the southern interest in maintaining the Jim Crow features of society were upheld.

The southern member throughout was Senator Allen Ellender of Louisiana. Ellender had established his reputation for racial reliability by opposing an anti-lynching bill in the wake of the Duck Hill lynchings of 1937. Anyone knowing the details of that lynching can have had little reason to doubt Ellender's reliability. He would remain with the housing bill throughout its legislative history, which lasted for more than three years.

The two main sponsors of the bill were northerners, as clear an indication as one might seek for the location of the problem they addressed. The problem was nearly entirely a northern and not a southern problem. From Cincinnati, Senator Robert Taft was shocked by conditions in the river city, especially in African American neighborhoods. Taft was a conservative but not a racist. He certainly had the intention to address the problem. The other main player was Senator Wagner from New York, a man of impeccable liberal credentials whose home state was being hit hardest by the migration.

Wagner may have been as significant as Senator Taft, but he was compelled to share the limelight with the building czar of New York City, the already legendary Robert Moses.[13] The great man had been busily constructing an independent power base since the opening of the Triborough Bridge in the mid-1930s. The bridge was paid for with federal money, and so independently of city and state. But the story is

Part One—The Regulatory Society

more complicated than these few words indicate and so is worth a brief digression.

In order to facilitate construction of the Triborough Bridge and its access roads, Moses created an authority independent of the state, the Triborough Bridge Authority (TBA), later the Triborough Bridge and Tunnel Authority (TBTA). Its financing came from bridge tolls, which returned more than a million dollars a day from the first day of the bridge's operation. Moses was free to use the money accrued for other projects, and so he did, constructing for example the Cross Bronx Expressway and the Brooklyn-Queens Expressway (BQE).[14]

Moses also used his considerable financing to hire lawyers who happened also to be city or state legislators to manage the insurance contracts for the bridge and its access roads, thereby insuring that he would get generous cooperation from city and state when it came to building public projects. Red warning flags went up in 1938 when New York State was revising its constitution, but not surprisingly, few serious incursions into Moses's power base were made.

Robert Moses moved on to become chief construction manager of a city project to provide homes for veterans returning after World War II. The project, called *Stuyvesant Town*, appeared at its start to be a public project, depending on the standards one uses to make such judgments. It became a private project when African American organizations demanded equal treatment for African American veterans. The story verges on embarrassment when the authorities (city and state) brought in the Metropolitan Life Insurance Company by granting the company remarkably generous tax abatements, a fig leaf that the New York state court upheld.

Nonetheless, it was thought that the experience of slum removal in creating Stuyvesant Town was invaluable. No other city in the Northeast had done anything remotely like Stuyvesant Town, and so it became the standard for how the 1949 Housing Act was meant to unfold. If this much made Robert Moses the point man for the legislation, then so much the better. For sure, Senator Taft thought that way. He knew Moses from before World War I, when they were college mates for three years at Yale in New Haven.

I would be remiss if I didn't confess that I don't know how many times Senator Taft and Robert Moses talked on the phone or through common friends.[15] If we settle for a consequentialist logic, meaning one in which we reason backwards from consequences to intentions, then

8. African American Exodus and the 1949 Housing Act

Taft and Moses had a great deal in common. In any case, Moses was given a good deal of authority to proceed with massive slum removal by Title 1 of the 1949 Housing Act, and as ever he was shovel-ready when the bill was signed into law.

The significance of Stuyvesant Town lay in its slum clearance aspect. The topic had been debated throughout the 1930s, when "Housers" like Catherine Bauer had opposed such an approach.[16] Their argument was that it was pointless to demolish so-called "slums" when land on the margins of the city was cheap and readily available. Nonetheless, a narrower mindset linked the existing tenements of New York's east side with opportunity because they could easily be demolished to make room for the new housing.

Whether Stuyvesant Town proved the validity of that argument is questionable, but not in doubt was that Moses presided over the largest demolition project in the history of New York City in order to get at the land on which Stuyvesant Town would be built. New York City had been the model for housing since Jacob Riis wrote *How the Other Half Lives* a half century earlier.[17] Riis had initiated the process of seeing the lower east side as a legendary slum, and so there was no turning away from New York City even before Moses arrived on the scene. But with Bob Moses in the saddle, which he was with the Stuyvesant Town project, there was as well no turning away to the alternative ideas of the Housers. Slum clearance was going to be the most disputed phase of the 1949 Housing Act.

❖ ❖ ❖

Not at first, but eventually, what became the 1949 Housing Act was known by the initials of its sponsors. At the beginning it was known as the WET bill, the initials standing for Wagner, Ellender, and Taft. Then with the upset victory of Republicans in the 1946 mid-term election it became known as the TEW bill, with Senator Taft moving from the rear to the front of the acronym. Then with Truman's upset victory in the 1948 election, the prospective legislation again became the WET bill, with Senator Wagner at the forefront.

In the entirety of this gestation period, the bill changed only by growing larger in order to meet a problem that was growing larger. When it was passed in final form in 1949, the Housing Act mandated the construction of more than 800,000 housing units (apartments) over a six year period, a vast number and a short time to do it in. If there were still states without housing agencies, they soon enough made up for the

Part One—The Regulatory Society

error of their ways. Nonetheless, the first of all housing agencies, the New York City Housing Authority (NYCHA), was the one best prepared to act first. It served as the model for the others that came after it.

The first action was not about housing but was rather about demolishing everything in sight. With a series of venal or incompetent New York mayors, the demolition was not difficult for Moses, who made certain that he was authorized to sell properties that did not fit in with his plans. Every other developer in New York City learned from Moses not so much how to profit but rather how the means, demolition in Moses case, was sanctioned by federal ends. Despite the shortcomings, New York under the informal leadership of Robert Moses quickly took the lead in the implementation of the 1949 Housing Act. Other states learned from New York and copied its methods, and so clearly New York was the state to watch in the 1950s.

Every day over the six years authorized by the 1949 legislation, Greyhound busses from cities in the South located along the Atlantic seaboard pulled into the future *Mid-Manhattan Bus Terminal,* where construction had started in the previous January and would continue until the terminal was completed in December 1950. Out of every bus spilled an inordinate number of African Americans, men and women with a number of children and a mess of luggage that had been dumped onto the loading platform. Sometimes the arrivals were met, but equally often they followed instructions in a letter they had been sent and made their way downstairs to take the "A" train uptown to Harlem or in a downtown direction and under the river to Brooklyn's Bedford Stuyvesant neighborhood, better known to New Yorkers as "Bed Stuy." In each place they doubled up in apartments cut into old brownstones and got the children into school.

The men soon enough tried to find jobs of any sort because the family seldom had enough money to even share the rent with their hosts. If they ever had a little extra cash, they bought bleacher tickets to major league ball games at Ebbets Field and saw Jackie Robinson play or to Yankee Stadium where Larry Doby made an occasional visit. If they had a sense of humor, they looked for the St. Louis Browns to come into town and hoped that Satchel Paige would pitch. But at all times they did what their preacher said and behaved themselves while taking seats in the bleachers.

The African Americans who increasingly filled Harlem and Bed-Stuy had few urban skills and hardly knew how to find their way to

8. African American Exodus and the 1949 Housing Act

the nearest subway stop and then around the city, but they were happy for one thing, which was that they were out of the agrarian South. Their counterparts who had changed buses at the Mid–Manhattan Bus Terminal and gone on to Boston or Cleveland in Ohio would not do better but would nonetheless find there a relative who knew how to talk them through the first weeks when hopefully the male in the family found some work and could chip in to pay the rent.

Back down South James Byrnes had just become governor of South Carolina and was listening closely to the white farmers who had got him elected. They told him that the exodus of African Americans was real and continuing and that he had to do something, anything, to keep them in Charleston and Columbia. A thorough racist, Byrnes determined to take *Plessy v. Ferguson* literally and make certain that African Americans got their fair share of public money. Byrnes may have been the first and last southerner who subscribed to the dictum "separate but equal" by giving the last word, *equal*, its due. Too late, however. South Carolina's African Americans continued to pour into Columbia and Charleston for one purpose only, which was to catch the next Greyhound bus out to Philly, New York, or Boston.

Not that it mattered, but Robert Moses in New York was not as fastidious as the former Secretary of State in South Carolina. Moses was collecting money now being channeled through the 1949 Housing Act and using it to tear down the slums near the docks on the East River south of 14th Street and down to East Broadway. It was Jews and not African Americans who were being displaced, but it didn't matter. The overall outcome for the city was a growing housing shortage, for Moses could not build as rapidly as he tore down, and he was determined to get slum clearance behind him before he put public housing in front of him. The 1950s were the decade when "Title 1," as the 1949 Housing Act was called, was fully implemented.

9

Explosion! Levittowns and Shopping Malls

A year after the GI Bill was amended to eliminate the down payment for veterans of the world war, a young building contractor named Bill Levitt was dutifully making his way around the small farms of eastern Long Island. He was making contingency purchases meant to work in tandem to assemble a single array of landholdings roughly the size of a small American township.[1]

At the time, tens of thousands of acres of Long Island's sandy land was dedicated to potato farming. Such land was poor for farming but excellent for building. The young building developer was himself a veteran. He had spent the war making military barracks built on slabs of poured concrete. On these, he assembled 2×4s, plywood, sheetrock, shingle-roofing, and milled windows into two-story buildings with outside staircases and entrances. All of that was Bill Levitt's contribution to saving the world from Hitler, Mussolini, and Tojo.

But in 1946 all of the above was the young developers past. In 1946, the young contractor was solely concerned with negotiating preliminary but binding agreements for Nassau County's many potato farms.[2] When Levitt began construction in 1947, his rough-cut township was named "Island Trees," and the homes were for rent, usually to working class families from nearby Brooklyn. At the time, blue-collar families were leaving the Brooklyn for the borough of Queens, and Levitt reasoned that he could pick off some of the overflow because his homes had a more rustic look than those being thrown up in Queens.

Levitt hired crews of workers, scores of them, and carefully arranged an assembly line that would be the admiration of Henry Ford. An initial crew set the re-bars and presided over cement trucks pouring pre-mixed cement into the molds. After three days of drying

9. Explosion! Levittowns and Shopping Malls

a second crew would come in with 2×4s and plywood as well as roofing materials to frame the building and protect the inside from rain. A day after they finished, a third crew would arrive on the scene to lay-in the wiring as well as the plumbing pipes. A fourth crew would install siding on the house as well as connect the stack to the sewage line in the street. Yet another crew would install doors and windows, followed by another to do the sheet-rocking and spackling. And so on it went, with each crew limited to a single skill that they applied repeatedly.

Starting in 1947 and in the manner described above, an average of 36 homes a day were completed. So things went for four years or until a reported 17,447 homes were completed, each varying minimally from the basic model. As demand grew, some design changes were added, the most significant being the addition of the "ranch" style to the basic "cape" of the original Island Trees.

What happened in 1947 then became the stuff of legend: many of the prospective renters were world war veterans who knew the fine print of the GI Bill, and so calculated that it would be not much more expensive to own than to rent. They repeatedly told Levitt as much, often in the form of an exclamation: "Boy, if you would sell me one of these babies, I'd buy it in an instant." Levitt listened and heard, but held his ground until March 1949, when he shifted to outright sales. The asking price was $7,990, which veterans could purchase without any down payment. On site, they could even negotiate a bank loan guaranteed by the government and spread over thirty years, thereby making the monthly cost about the same as renting an apartment in nearby Brooklyn.

The purchase of a home came accompanied with a written guarantee of racial compatibility, which when translated into plain English meant that African Americans were excluded from Levittown. There were a few African American veterans who were interested and who did qualify for the loans guaranteed by their government, namely those that were fixed-rate, twenty to thirty years in duration, insured, but they were firmly steered away from purchases at Levittown.

Ugly scenes did not happen. Interested African Americans, it there were any who persisted, did not come to the Sunday open houses. Instead, and by word of mouth, they were steered in the direction of the nearby hamlet of Roosevelt, Uniondale, and the larger township of Hempstead. There they were told they could find something similar

Part One—The Regulatory Society

to what was denied them in Levittown. Without the necessary coping skills, they complied.

And so, by 1950 and on the wider spread of land that was greater New York City, a remarkable social change was taking place. Both whites and blacks were on the move, whites out of the city and blacks into sections called Harlem in Manhattan and Bed-Stuy in Brooklyn. At the time, few persons argued that if this kind of arrangement continued for five more years, New York City would be changed irrevocably.

Notoriously, and as if to confirm the above estimate, Walter O'Malley was on the brink of deciding to move the Brooklyn Dodgers baseball team to Los Angeles. According to local legend, if O'Malley would consider remaining, Robert Moses was willing to build him a new stadium in Flushing, Queens, adjacent to highways leading to and from Levittown on the Island. The message was clear: Ebbets Field was being surrounded by Negro neighborhoods, and so Moses was offering O'Malley a venue that was chiefly reachable by automobile. O'Malley was willing to stay, but only with a new stadium in Brooklyn and not in Flushing. Moses persisted and so O'Malley headed west. Moses eventually succeeded, but only with an expansion team: the Mets. The old Ebbets Field was torn down and public housing paid for through the 1949 Housing Act was put in its place.

And so by the 1950s, something was happening that would change the character of New York City irrevocably. Blacks were migrating out of the South and into the city. Whites were migrating to Queens and out of the city into the suburbs, with Levittown the talisman for the movement. The Dodgers, the boys of summer, were out and the "incredibles" were in. The reigning opinion was that New York City was a lost cause.

◆◆◆

African Americans were also migrating to California, albeit in much smaller numbers than to the Upper Midwest and to coastal cities like New York. Not so whites. Where World War I had been fought against a single enemy in Europe, World War II was fought against enemies opposite both coasts. Consequently, aircraft factories, shipyards, supply depots, and military bases sprang up on the West Coast as well as on the east coast, and with them well-paying jobs. Whites flocked west, either in or out of uniform, headed for workplaces and bases in Oakland, Long Beach, and San Diego.

9. Explosion! Levittowns and Shopping Malls

It was obvious that in California a postwar housing market for veterans would blossom, and so while Bill Levitt was purchasing and assembling the land that would become Levittown, his western counterparts were doing something similar in respect to farms just north of the port of Long Beach. The developers were Louis Boyar, Mark Taper, and Ben Weingart, all with ideas uncannily similar to Bell Levitt's. Their disqualification as originators of the automobile suburb was to have begun their project after Levitt had begun his. Their advantage was that many Californians had heard of Levittown and so knew what to expect when Lakewood was opened to the public on March 24, 1950. An estimated 30,000 persons came to see the seven model homes on the first day the project was open. Within five weeks, 1,000 homes had been sold, most to young veterans. In the next three years, 17,500 homes were built and sold, a number nearly identical to that of Levittown in New York.

Developers are everywhere cut from the same cloth, and so things went according to the Levittown model outside every city in the United States. By 1960, suburbs grew 50 percent larger in population than they had been in 1950. Growth in the number of television sets in the same period was equally remarkable. Only 12 percent of American families owned a television in 1950. By 1960 that number was up to 75 percent. Shows grew accordingly, and so where the viewing public for Sid Caesar in 1949 was small, it was correspondingly larger for the Lucille Ball show in 1955 and even larger for "Bringing Up Father" in 1960. The 1950s projected an aura of progress that was overwhelming to those who experienced it. Putting tailfins and wrap-around windshields on cars seemed only the right thing to do, as did taking an airplane flight or having the Dodgers and Giants make California their home.

My experience as a small child mirrored the description of the previous paragraph and so was representative of what was happening across the nation. The town fathers if Chicopee, Massachusetts, started by getting state authorities to fund a new highway that would be a memorial to the soldiers and sailors of no particular war, one that was appropriately called *Memorial Drive*. As soon as the highway was mapped out, developers moved in to imitate the feat of Bill Levitt in Nassau County by buying out adjacent garden farmers. No one asked where our vegetables would come from. We had faith that the Blessed Virgin would take care of us.

A pair of developers surnamed Keddy and Vadnais bought a small

Part One—The Regulatory Society

farm on Pendleton Avenue, just off Memorial Drive, and announced plans to build 57 ranch homes of varying sizes. They were actually all identical but varied according to the additions one tacked on. My parents went the whole way and got a garage with an attached "breezeway." They bought the property in 1953 and then drove by every Sunday to view the builder's progress in putting up their castle. They, or I should say "we" moved to the place in August 1954. Our neighbors soon enough moved in, and since everyone was pleased with themselves for having had the wisdom to be the first suburbanites, they were also pleased with each other, and also generally pleasing. If anyone read Galbraith's *Affluent Society* when it appeared in 1958, that in itself was news. Everyone was too busy having cookouts.

Memorial Drive was punctuated by crossing roads with intersections designed as rotaries so that traffic signals could be eliminated. Between the first and second rotaries, just after the new gasoline station but before the new supermarket, lay our arrangement. What we experienced was replicated one-thousand times, so much so that I later learned to think of highways as natural arteries and only wished there was more of them. In school we were taught that the highways were necessary for our defense against the Soviet Union. Everywhere I went in the late 1960s, I somehow managed to arrive at a home similar to mine, and everyone was always having cookouts.

The only thing missing from my parents' home was the opportunity to concentrate one's shopping in one place, as they could do in Lakewood, California, or at a place called Edina in Minnesota. These phenomena were called "shopping malls," and unfortunately I cannot remember when I experienced my first one, but without question there was a day one.

※ ※ ※

Much later I learned what these meccas of consumerism were and how they developed, but initially I had no idea that there were developers behind them as well. The first and greatest of such geniuses was an Austrian expatriate named Victor Gruen, whose name at birth was *Viktor Gruenbaum*. He was an Austrian Jew who had learned architecture at the same institute that had rejected Adolf Hitler. Gruenbaum had the good sense to leave Vienna on the same day Hitler decided to move back in. Gruenbaum continued his migration and so arrived in the United States with eight dollars in his pocket and no command of English. He

9. Explosion! Levittowns and Shopping Malls

was a skilled draftsman, however, a skill that enabled him to pay the rent and put food on the table during the war years.

After the war, Gruenbaum, now Gruen, contracted to develop the dreary downtown of Kalamazoo, Michigan, an experience that might have struck him for its sheer artificiality but apparently didn't. Gruen then got a contract to develop a place named Edina in Minnesota, mentioned earlier. Called the "Southdale Center," its truly distinguishing feature was that the shops faced inward toward each other rather than outward toward parking lots. It was now only a short step to have Gruen persuade the town fathers to put a roof over the arrangement and add air-conditioning and some of those drapes with icicles on them to communicate that it was a different world inside.

By the dozens, then scores, then hundreds, enclosed shopping malls were built across the United States. They were wildly popular and so became destinations for Americans, or rather places where they were happy to spend the day, including time out for dining at one of the fast-food restaurants that specialized in hamburgers, French fries, and "shakes." The arrangement at Edina was typical in being anchored at both ends by leading department stores from Minneapolis, with hundreds of shops between the two anchors.

Gruen was smitten by an idea he understood to be the *public space*, an idea that he had learned back in Vienna where the *Ringstrasse* was dotted with historical sites to remind strollers that it was not just a commercial thoroughfare.[3] The statues of the Vienna street would later be deemed to be *historicist*, which is to say, referring to history but without the context, without the actual history. This gave the *Ringstrasse* an arbitrary character, which to many would seem manipulative. But not to Victor Gruen, who thought of the *Ringstrasse* as the ultimate public space, much in the way many of us continue to think of art museums as the ultimate art spaces.

Victor Gruen persuaded himself that his shopping malls were protean public spaces, complete in all but some final touches. His vision of a public space was not so much a Roman forum thronged with citizens eager to hear Caesar orate but was rather more focused on the core element of discourse between two interlocutors. That such discourse might take the form of conversation struck him as natural, and so he featured the cafe with tables and chairs as a necessary element of every shopping mall he designed. Department stores at both ends were the twin anchors, but a cafe somewhere in between was the civic center.

Part One—The Regulatory Society

The reader might guess that Gruen was disappointed when collections of shoppers converged on his cafe and besides ordering burgers and fries showed themselves most eager to display to each other what they had acquired at one of the shops on the mall. Such persons showed themselves to be consumers throughout, for not only did they buy and use objects at the mall, but they also identified with the objects. "That dress is you, Dorothy, you every step of the way. It's got you written all over it." Such identification showed what commercial society was about: it was a matter of providing identification to persons who otherwise did not have one. The fictional "Dorothy" was a person who would not have been born had their not been an aircraft factory or automobile assembly plant to provide her parents with the income to have and raise children.

But Gruen apparently expected Dorothy to rise to the occasion and launch an oration for the others at the table eating their burgers and fries. Disappointed, Gruen went so far as to leave behind his acquired American citizenship and return to the Austria of the *Ringstrasse*, where stony historical figures decorating fountains and announcing buildings continued to point the way forward in time for contemporaries.

Arguably Gruen merits the accolade Malcolm Gladwell bestows on Gruen as the 20th century's most significant architect.[4] Gruen continued to understand pubis space in the manner of an intellectual who deems culture-laden Europe to be superior to a stripped-down and materialistic America. While that stance contains a shadow of truth, it also masks the reality of a commodified culture that hides its materialism behind illusions that enable Europeans to feel superior only to more stripped-down versions of their own phantasies.

One finds a healthier realism in the Secessionist architecture of Otto Wagner as well as in Michael Sorkin's edited *Theme Park: The New American City and the End of Public Space*.[5] Entertainment, as implied in the term "theme park," is what could be achieved and was indeed actually featured by Gruen's great competitor in Florida, *Walt Disney World* does not just add themes, as does the *Ringstrasse*. It instead makes the theme the center of its being, thereby luring in an enthusiastic middle class that would prefer to make the themed ride the center of the day's activities rather than an add-on at the end of a long day's shopping.

Gruen's phantasy was of a cafe in which a small group of European intellectuals gathered around a stony figure and celebrated the triumphal conclusion of European culture. He never did grasp that Viennese such as Karl Krauss were lamenting rather than celebrating the

9. Explosion! Levittowns and Shopping Malls

achievements of their culture. Sigmund Freud was telling us how far we had descended from the words of Pericles to the deeds of modern hysterics.

There is a certain measure of superiority to American over European civilization, namely its greater honesty in resisting the nonsense of European art. The cookie-cutter "capes" of Levittown do just that, as does the stripped-down shopping centers of 1950s Detroit. They confront us with the real conditions of our existence.

Part Two

The Deregulated Society

10

The White Working Class and the "Treaty of Detroit"

To understand the so-called Treaty of Detroit, it is first necessary to understand the American working class and its labor leaders. Let me take them one at a time, and separately before bringing them together.

Detroit's working class in the first decade of the last century was mainly comprised of skilled workers. It was Henry Ford who decided, or discovered, that with enough expansion at his Highland Park factory, he could rationalize the labor process and welcome less expensive unskilled workers, mainly from the agrarian South, as well as from Eastern Europe. By 1920, or the time Ford moved to the River Rouge complex of factories, Ford's labor force had changed radically. It was predominantly white, unskilled, from Eastern Europe, and from the South (of the U.S. and not just Europe). Inexperienced, it was skeptical of unionization.

When World War I ended, the chief organized union was the International Workers of the World, abbreviated as the IWW and more familiar as the "Wobblies." Beside them stood the American Federation of Labor, an umbrella organization of multiple skilled unions losing ground in proportion as the labor force was being deskilled. Throwing a chill over everything was the distant Russian Revolution. It gave heart to local communists despite their inability to gain traction among Detroit's various labor communities. It frightened everyone else. But as the 1920s progressed, it became clearer that the major division within American labor was not between communists and more democratically inclined socialists but rather between skilled and unskilled workers.

Due to Henry Ford's 1913 actions, so-called "unskilled" workers were becoming increasingly significant. Consequently, there arose within the American Federation of Labor (AFL) a countermovement that sought to organize workers not on the basis of skills but rather on the basis of the industry they were employed in. The countermovement would eventually split with the AFL and come to be called the Congress of Industrial Organizations, or the CIO.

Alongside this developing split, another question, every bit as basic, was being posed. Why was there no socialism in the United States? That question, posed by a visiting German sociologist in 1906, amounted to asking why there was no political dimension to American labor, for socialism, if it ever existed in the United States, could only be the product of state policy.[1] Anything less was utopian and would not work, as had been demonstrated repeatedly in the 19th century. The split between AFL and CIO, however interesting, did not resolve the question why there was no political dimension to organized American labor.

At this point I want to avoid misunderstanding by posing the question in the most obvious terms. Of course, American labor unions were interested in what the state, national or local, did with labor questions, but short of having a political party, they could do nothing but lobby in respect to the questions they shared with the state. German unions were represented by a political party, the SPD, as were British unions with the Labour Party. But alone among all the forces of organized labor in the most advanced Western countries, the American unions had no political party to represent it.

The consequence of such a deficiency was that American labor, by which I mean the most basic blue-collar laborers, tended to seek private solutions and avoid any solutions that were or just seemed public. The latter were deemed to be *socialistic*, by which was meant that they were supplied by the state.

What else could state solutions be except social in the sense that they were for classifications of persons—women, children, the elderly, the unemployed, veterans—and not for individuals? That definitional requirement didn't matter, however. They were still social, a term that easily mutated into *socialistic*, and usually without further explanation.

To the objection that such an argument was absurd, that a non-state entity like the Ford Motor Company also provided solutions to problems that were social, applying for example to unskilled workers as a category and not to individuals, there was no response. Ford could do as much without objection, and so when workers were seeking collective solutions, they would do better to go to a corporation than to the state.

10. The White Working Class and the "Treaty of Detroit"

When one ponders this situation, it reveals itself to be absurd. The American state is the creation of the people—*We the people*—and so going to that collective source for a collective solution is indeed "social" without there being anything "socialistic" about it. When we pause and ask where this slander of being "socialistic" originated, the most likely answer is with the 1917 Russian Revolution and the American law that most directly reacted to it: the 1918 Sedition Act. The modern American Book of Matthew, as it were, is the period just after the war when A. Mitchell Palmer was Attorney General. The American crucifixion scene is the arrest and imprisonment of Eugene Debs. His Pontius Pilate was none other than Woodrow Wilson.

I have no intention of dwelling on events so distant from the 1950 Treaty of Detroit, for it tells a similar story only more directly. Here we have a primal event of generic quality, namely, the unionized working class seeking its salvation not from the state but rather from a corporation. The legitimacy of the Treaty of Detroit depended entirely on no one shouting that what this agreement provided was socialism, or to be more specific, socialized medicine, even though it was just that. Senator McCarthy was waiting in the wings, but neither he nor anyone else pointed the finger and claimed the 1950 agreement was socialism. Apparently, what was good for General Motors was indeed good for the nation.

The answer to the question posed earlier—"Why is there no socialism in the United States of America"—is that the question itself is misguided.[2] There was and is plenty of socialism in the United States of America. What's missing is the state, not the socialism, and the New Deal had done little to change that. The so-called Treaty of Detroit was and remains the most stunning example of socialism being provided without the state being involved. As a consequence, it presents a problem, and one of immense proportions, for the Treaty of Detroit taught an example, and one still being followed. I take up that theme in the balance of this chapter.

❖❖❖

Walter Reuther and then his brother arrived in Detroit in 1927, making his way to that city with the idea of becoming a *tool and die* maker, to use the common composite term to describe the only occupation at the Ford company that was not subjected to deskilling pressures.[3] Reuther learned the skills and eventually signed up to work under a Ford

Part Two—The Deregulated Society

contract that required them to reassemble the old dies that had stamped out the parts of Model Ts.

The catch was that the job was at an expanded facility at Nizhni Novgorod (Gorky) in the Soviet Union. The brothers eventually left for Europe, saw Hitler's Germany as well as Western Europe, found their way to Gorky, spent something more than a year transmitting their skills to Soviet workers, and eventually returned to Detroit in 1935. Within months they were involved in an embryonic trade union called the United Automobile Workers, or UAW.

The signature characteristic of the new UAW was organizing workers on an industry basis rather than on the basis of skills. The fledgling union was inclined to become a member of the similarly conceived Congress of Industrial Organizations, or CIO, and not the older AFL. Within a year, the fledgling union was engaged in organizing laborers in Flint outside Detroit, where a GM facility that made and stored dies was located. Reuther was marginal to the events in Flint.

In the last day of 1936, push came to shove when word arrived that GM was going to occupy the key die making facility in order to protect it. The union decided to act first by occupying the building. It did so and then refused to leave.[4] That was the beginning of the 1937 Flint Sit-Down Strike, a critically important move because the strikers were inside rather than outside the facility being struck. The company was frozen in place for fear that the strikers would destroy the valuable dies in the building if GM's security force invaded. A similar reasoning applied to the police.

The rest is history, so it is said, but nonetheless that rest is still worth covering to bring this chapter up to the Treaty of Detroit. Once the UAW had negotiated a satisfactory contract with General Motors, the other automobile makers, Ford and Chrysler, promptly fell into line. This meant recognizing the union as the sole bargaining agent for their workers and initialing similar contracts. As this happened, droves of automotive workers lined up to join the UAW, not only in Detroit but also along the complicated supply chain that serviced the so-called Big Three. Hence, similar contracts were signed with workers making tires in Akron, automotive glass in Toledo, and rolled-steel in Youngstown—all three cities in Ohio.

While all this was happening, the president was shifting his gaze to Europe and the Far East in preparation for war. Union leaders supported

10. The White Working Class and the "Treaty of Detroit"

the change and helped hold the UAW in check for the sake of a unified home front, forsaking strikes and allowing grievances to accumulate. By the end of 1944 it was clear that the war overseas had been won by the allies and that it was time for unions to return to normalcy at home. Reuther was not even the head of the UAW, never mind the larger CIO, but still it was time for him and other labor leaders to define their positions.

※ ※ ※

The period 1945–1950 in American labor relations is riddled with negotiations and strikes, accusations of communism, political shifts to the right (as in the 1946 mid-term elections), and anti-union legislation such as the Taft-Hartley Act. Such events threatened the party with a regional split. But then, defying all odds, the upset 1948 Truman victory enabled the *Fair Deal* to gain a footing, and finally the 1949 Housing Act.

For a while it looked as though the world was coming to an end, but then the sun rose, at least *a* sun in the form of a breakthrough labor agreement initialed by General Motors (GM) on one side of the table and Walter Reuther for the United Automobile Workers (UAW) on the other side. Within weeks, it was labeled the *Treaty of Detroit* by *Fortune* magazine, and as such it entered labor history as the culmination of a half-century of struggle and the beginning of a decade long plateau during which labor rode on the crest of a wave from one success to the next.

What was the "Treaty of Detroit," and was it up to being what it was cracked up to be? I will begin the second half of this book by arguing my opinion on what was, after all, little more than the momentary meeting ground of two factors of production, capital and labor, and as such an understanding that would last only for as long of the two sides allowed it to last. So what was it, this Treaty of Detroit?

First, its terms: the 1950 agreement between GM and the UAW included clauses ceding moderate pay raises to the company's assemblers. More significant were the clauses dealing with fringe benefits, especially health and retirement benefits. GM agreed to partially cover medical expenses for qualified workers and their families for the period when workers were active as well as for their retirement. In return, the union agreed not to strike or to conduct actions that were the equivalent of strikes, like slowdowns. Although Reuther ha a position on

Part Two—The Deregulated Society

automobile pricing, he nonetheless also agreed to cede policymaking in respect to pricing and modeling to management.

The contract had the immediate effect of inducing the other two Detroit automobile makers, Ford and Chrysler, to save the money that would be spent on legal fees for negotiating settlements with the same union by going through the motions but quickly settling on similar if not identical terms. The model then spread like a virus down the automotive supply-chain, for example to automotive glassmakers in Toledo, Ohio, and to tire makers in Akron, Ohio.

By 1950, the supply-chain of the automotive industry had become more complicated than most persons realized. In the 1920s at the Rouge complex of plants, Ford had made its own steel. By 1950 that operation was no more as Ford and the other two auto makers were buying rolled steel from Cleveland, Pittsburgh, and Youngstown. Some of that steel was shipped to intermediary industries, for example to the Moore Drop Forging Company in Springfield, Massachusetts, which had a contract to make drop-forged brake and clutch pedals for Ford vehicles. Unions organizing workers at the Moore factories then had to negotiate their own contracts with Moore Drop Forging, and they could think of nothing better to do than say, "Why not us too?" as they asked for terms similar to those of the Treaty of Detroit.

The long and short of the story is that the Treaty of Detroit had a ripple effect that ran through the whole American economy, and to make matters more complicated for management, Reuther had insisted that the company not raise the base price of automobiles as a consequence of the contract. That clause also rippled across the American economy, with workers getting more of the rewards and management less. The overall outcome was a reduction of inequality in American society, a phenomenon that did not resonate in the press because less inequality (or greater equality) did not appear to be an issue worth reporting.

By 1955, five years after the Treaty of Detroit was initialed, any blue-collar worker who could hold his drink and keep his marriage intact was living in a two-bedroom ranch or split-level, driving a Ford or Chevy, having backyard cookouts, taking vacations up by the lake, and thinking about moving up to a Mercury, Dodge, or Olds because of the wrap-around windows and the tailfins. *Laissez-rouler le bon temps*, said the mayor of New Orleans, and they sure did.

◆◆◆

10. The White Working Class and the "Treaty of Detroit"

Through the postwar years, Walter Reuther indicated a desire to lead or be involved in any initiative resulting in a political party that approximated social democracy in its policies and impulses. Along with Eleanor Roosevelt, Reuther was a founding member of Americans for Democratic Action (ADA) and supportive of other such groups interested in changing American political culture on the ground. Like the former president's widow, Reuther was skeptical of the motives of Harry Truman, considering him weak and dependent upon the support of party hacks. They failed to see in Truman any redeeming virtues and so were determined to make a new political beginning.

The victory of party liberals in backing a liberal racial plank at the Democratic Party's 1948 convention, the break-out of Strom Thurmond as well as the founding of the Dixiecrats, and the unexpected victory of Truman in the 1948 election came as a surprise, even a shock, to the founding generation of the ADA. In the moment of political triumph, all thoughts of founding an American Labor Party were banished from their heads. The moment had passed, and so too imaginings of a third political party.

To pinpoint a beam of light on Reuther, could he or should he have acted in the period 1945 to 1950, understanding the latter as two separate periods linked by the improbable 1948 election. Should Reuther have acted after the Republicans' 1946 mid-term election victory, with Truman set back on his heels? Or should they have acted when given a second chance, after the improbable 1948 presidential election victory, when the Democrats also controlled both houses of Congress and the southern delegation had been rebuffed in the 1948 election? The answers will be speculative, but they should nonetheless be aired out.

The argument for acting during the period after the 1946 mid-term election is that Republicans were hell-bent on gutting the Wagner Act and New Deal supporters were on their heels. The problem for Reuther, however, was that he was far from being in control of a union that was growing faster than his career was advancing. Such growth was not so much about the union was increasing its number of workers as it was about the union and it members growing wealthier. Such Americans were hungry for automobiles and so Detroit's factories were working three shifts to keep up with demand. Workers' wallets were bulging. Many were also taking advantage of the GI Bill to buy homes, and those who were not veterans were not much worse off for their reliance on the financial guarantees of the 1934 Housing Act.

Part Two—The Deregulated Society

The UAW had grown astronomically in the ten years since the 1937 Flint Sit-Down strike.

The 1950 Treaty of Detroit then gave to workers something they had not bargained for, to pun a phrase. Bargaining tended to favor wage increases, with the issue of health benefits existing more as an item on a wish-list that was unlikely to be recognized as legitimate, never mind agreed to and funded. Then came the prolonged negotiations of 1950 the give-and-take of which tended steadily in the direction of recognizing the legitimacy of the issue of health coverage. General Motors was willing to talk about it.

Health coverage is a term that begs to be more precisely defined. Who is and is not covered? Certainly the worker, but his family as well? That has to be negotiated. And then just what is covered? Certainly illness and necessary surgery, but surgery for medical conditions present before the employee's tenure at the company. Called pre-existing conditions, that issue too had to be negotiated. For what duration was the coverage? Certainly for as long as the worker was employed by the firm, but for retirement as well? And when does such coverage kick in, which is to say, when does the worker become vested? After five, ten, or twenty years on the company's employment roles? These and other issues had to be negotiated.

But every issue raised above skirts the main issue, which has to do with the role of the state. That issue had been introduced into politics in 1888 when Bismarck unilaterally proposed health coverage for categories of German industrial workers. The coverage was limited and medicine was relatively inexpensive, but that was all beside the point that Bismarck was thought to be the least likely figure to propose such an initiative. Ten years earlier he had succeeded in outlawing the German socialist party, thereby establishing him as no friend of organized labor.

But Bismarck was from the agrarian east of Germany and he needed allies in the industrialized western provinces. What better move than to propose the measure most desired by socialists and hated by employers. The secret, which everyone was aware of, was that the state could negotiate lower costs for medical care and also spread the costs over the entire population. Nonetheless, despite every rationalization, his was a daring politics, and it resonated across Europe.

England may not have been the first place Bismarck's medical reforms resonated, but they certainly made a mark there. The agrarian classes were beginning to suffer under rising land taxes, eventually

10. The White Working Class and the "Treaty of Detroit"

called "death" taxes. Manufacturers were afraid they could not afford to cede any ground on the issue, and so medical coverage of workers was firmly shoved to the side. Its role, however, was significant, for it made union leaders put it on their agenda, where it became a source of demands.

In Germany, meanwhile, the socialist party was reinstated. It used the opportunity to change its name to the Social Democratic Party of Germany, better known by its initials as the SPD. The name-change, from socialist to social democratic, reflected an internal debate roiling Germany. The debate was led by Eduard Bernstein, who in 1899 had published *Evolutionary Socialism*, whose argument was directed against revolutionary Marxism, which at the time had devolved into a theoretical position advocated by most of the leaders of the German SPD. The gist of Bernstein's argument was that capitalism was evolving toward greater worker rights, established informally and sometimes, as was the case with Bismarck's health care reforms, guaranteed by the state. The working class would do better to go in this direction, cultivating reforms and honing their class consciousness.

We have no way of knowing if Walter Reuther had ever read Eduard Bernstein, but we do know from speeches and writings that from 1945 to 1950 Reuther favored the emergence of social democracy and the development of working-class consciousness. The problem is that these remained undeveloped impulses on Reuther's part. He did not take time out to think and write about such matters. He instead worked for proximate goals, like organizing workers and preparing strikes. He supported the efforts of others to develop social democracy but nonetheless recognized these as episodic and so lacking a systematic character.

Hence, at all times leading up to the Treaty of Detroit, Reuther said the right things but did not act on them. In effect, Reuther was not like Eduard Bernstein or even Rosa Luxembourg, the first writing a book on Marxism and the second a book to refute it. They were what Americans were once fond of calling European intellectuals, but in fact that has always been a way of kicking them upstairs. What it meant was that American labor leaders were always too busy with the questions of the day to take up such arcane matters as the role of the state in worker welfare or the development of class consciousness. If there was such a thing as *false consciousness*, it was not only a characteristic of most American labor leaders but also a characteristic of Walter Reuther as well.

It is therefore that Reuther did not act to make the state the

Part Two—The Deregulated Society

guarantor of workers' health, more or less in the manner Franklin D. Roosevelt had acted to make it the guarantor of housing in the 1934 Housing Act. But however much Roosevelt might appear to be a second Bismarck, he was not, for the housing being given the financial guarantees of the government was more or less tailor designed to make workers into property-owners and so possessors of an untrustworthy consciousness.

And this was precisely the condition of workers in 1950 in Detroit. It cannot be said that automotive assemblers loved their new health care benefits more than they loved their new split-levels, but on the basis of intuition it can be said that the Treaty of Detroit made them more beholden to the company than ever before. Every such effort failed, and if we are to believe Nelson Lichtenstein, Reuther's biographer, and the failure was traceable to inadequate social consciousness.[5]

11

Brown, Civil Rights and the End of the New Deal

Social historians like to pick out and privilege a narrative that might better have remained in a tapestry of social movements. Such is the case with the African American civil rights movement, which offers a number of points from which to view it but is often grossly simplified. The conflicting positions of Booker T. Washington and W.E.B. Du Bois in the early part of the century, the role of lynchings like that of Emmett Till in 1955, or the breaking down of race barriers in professional sports—these are all plausible starting points.

They are not where I would begin my version of this key narrative, however. My choice would be to begin in 1944 with the publication of Gunnar Myrdal's *An American Dilemma: The Negro Problem and Modern Democracy*. The reason for that choice is simple.[1] The Swedish sociologist offered a perspective that contextualized all the others. Myrdal argued for piecemeal school integration as the preferred method of creating an integrated society out of one that had been artificially segregated by Jim Crow laws. Let children of different races play with each other and all frozen social barriers would begin to melt. Provide a generation of such *Kindergarten* beginnings and the segregated society would become integrated.

The NAACP paid heed and under the guidance of Thurgood Marshall began testing the waters with carefully selected cases like *Sweatt v. Painter*, a 1950 Texas case that challenged the unreasonableness of segregation at the most advanced educational level.[2] If there were any remaining doubts about how the NAACP was proceeding, they were dispelled In the same year when *McLaurin v Oklahoma State Regents*

Part Two—The Deregulated Society

questioned integration when segregation was practiced within an integrated facility.[3] The two cases clearly indicated where the Supreme Court was heading in entertaining these arguments. In 1954 and with *Brown v. Bd. of Education of Topeka* the court came face-to-face with Myrdal's dilemma.[4] In a unanimous vote, it decided to order the desegregation of the nation's schools, and a year later it mandated that such schools should be integrated with "all deliberate speed."

In the same year the Court decided *Brown* and at the University of Virginia a scholar named C. Vann Woodward delivered a series of lectures on the legal background of segregation. One year later, 1955, Woodward published *The Strange Career of Jim Crow*, an expanded version of those lectures.[5] With the case and the book, the legal strategy had the basis for expanding into a civil rights movement on the ground. That movement began in December 1955 when Rosa Parks refused to give up her seat to a white person on a Montgomery, Alabama, city bus.[6] The Montgomery bus boycott was thereafter led by Martin Luther King, Jr., and it lasted for nearly all of 1956.

The civil rights movement might have ended with the success of the Montgomery bus boycott, but Dr. King had put together a team and hence was open to additional cases to which he might apply his talents. At this point King ran up against the doubts of Ella Baker, an African American woman who despite her doubts supported Dr. King wholeheartedly.[7]

But with Ella Baker's doubts, the civil rights movement began to take on a dual character, probably beginning to do so as early as 1958. On one side of the duality was the Southern Christian Leadership Conference (SCLC) chaired by King and organized around black churches, their predominantly female members and their predominantly male leaders.[8] On the other side of the duality, were the activist students involved in grassroots efforts and not characterized by any outstanding leaders and giving little of the deference commanded by the Reverend Dr. King.

The first of these alternative leaders was Stokely Carmichael of the Student Nonviolent Coordinating Committee (SNCC). He was followed by H. Rap Brown. Despite the second term of the SNCC's name—Nonviolent—the student leaders fully embraced the prospect of violence, not so much because they wanted it as because they expected to be the victims of it. With this kind of appraisal of the internal situation of American politics, the first great internal division of the civil rights movement

11. Brown, Civil Rights and the End of the New Deal

was revealed for all who cared to see it. To be candid about the situation, it was in the interest of African Americans to be non-violent but by the same token was in the interest of their opposition to be violent.

As the focal point of civil rights protest, the North began to replace the South in 1966. It did so when the civil rights movement in Chicago became the successor to the civil rights movement that had peaked a year earlier in Selma, Alabama.[9] Where voting had been the issue in Selma, housing became the frontal issue in the suburb of North Lawndale west of downtown Chicago. That fact does not always appear to be the case, but that it was so became clear when the response in Congress became the 1968 Fair Housing Act, by consensus the third legislative leg of the civil rights movement.[10] The first two laws were the Civil Rights Act of 1964 and the Voting Rights Act of 1965. The third leg was the 1968 Fair Housing Act, but how the nation got there has long remained unclear.

To better understand the situation in Chicago, a pair of imaginary maps depicting the two great migrations of the 20th century is needed. Beryl Satter understood as much and at least for Chicago included such maps in her book, *Family Properties, Race, Real Estate, and the Exploitation of Black Urban America*.[11] The first map clearly shows that the Great Migration of the World War I period placed African Americans on a strip of neighborhoods stretching southwards from the city's center in the loop. The second and much larger Great Migration located African Americans not only in the city's Southside neighborhoods but also saw them push out westwards to Garfield Park and toward the city's western boundary.

In *Lawn*, a generic term I will use for all the affected westerly neighborhoods, there was no nearby assembly factory of automobiles or tractors and so no clear way to identify the occupants as members of a manufacturing class. The neighborhood had recently been populated by immigrants from eastern and southern Europe, most of whom were smitten by the American dream and so reluctant to flee at the first whiff of "invasion by" aliens. If one wanted an example of a red-lined neighborhood, Lawn was it. Lawn was nowhere near to being called a slum by developers, but it was characterized by enough social instability to merit the notorious designation.

The real estate situation was characterized by a procedure called *contract sales*. The latter worked as follows: white property owners in western suburbs like Lawn were nervous about African Americans

Part Two—The Deregulated Society

moving into the neighborhoods and lowering property values. Neighborhood banks tended to red line the neighborhood and deny mortgages to increasingly African American applicants. Self-appointed real estate agents fanned these embers as part of a sales pitch keyed to buying the homes for discounted prices, all cash of course, and with immediate closings. These might best be called "contract-purchases," although to the best of my knowledge they were not.

Assume a single family property was worth $50,000 at the time, the early 1960s. The agent would lament the neighborhood situation but reluctantly offer the homeowner $35,000 cash, with an immediate closing because no investigation of the agent's credit was involved. This was a big loss for a homeowner who expected to finance his retirements from the home's sale, but still was pretty good given the assumed reality on the ground.

Once the couple had settled with the agent and moved out, the agent would bring in a prospective African American couple and offer them the same home for $75,000, with 50 percent down and the balance financed in a mortgage arranged by the agent through his connections to so-called "hard-money" men. The contract assigned the agent the right to repossess the home if the client were more than a day late on paying the monthly mortgage. Tough terms, admittedly, but if the couple could do better at the local bank, then by all means they should try.

On the assumption that African American homeowners were not backed up by savings and were insecure in their employment, the chances were high that the couple would default at some point within the first few years, in which case the agent (or his agent) would pounce and repossess the home, adhering to the literal wording of the contract and evicting the couple on the spot and on the same day.

After an interval for emotions to cool, the original agent or more likely a different agent he had passed the property to would arrive with another African American couple interested in buying the home for $90,000. The story would then unfold as above, or with luck the African American couple would have back-up finances for the inevitable rainy day.

Already interesting, the story becomes more so when it mutates into politics, for what is required of the state, in this case the Illinois Attorney General or the Cook County District Attorney, is a set of lending regulations that are effectively enforced and known to be so. The creation of such a legal safety net is also dependent on the good will

11. Brown, Civil Rights and the End of the New Deal

of the governor or the mayor. If the latter is lacking or the governor or mayor are outright opposed to such regulations, then the legal system may be checked or even checkmated. Chicago Mayor Daley usually had the right ideas, but insofar as his campaign chest was filled with donations from real estate interests, he may also have been slow in implementing those ideas.

The Chicago Freedom Movement of the mid–1960s was something less than fully successful, but it nonetheless had echoes nationally and so resulted in Congress passing the 1968 Fair Housing Act.[12] The latter was a well-meaning law passed a week after the assassination of Martin Luther King, Jr. But the national legislation entailed further enabling legislation at the state level. The Chicago Freedom Movement may thus be judged the first but not the last named event in a more prolonged civil rights movement for fair housing.

As such, the Chicago Freedom Movement is another term for the evolving American consumer society, for until 1966, African Americans wanting to purchase homes were relegated to suburban ghettoes like Roosevelt on Long Island or Levittown in New Jersey, which later changed its name to Willingboro, New Jersey. In 1966, with the help of Dr. Martin Luther King, Jr., and on a major scale, African Americans were attempting to crack the white suburbs. It was a major moment in civil rights history, and for this book is a major turning point in the history of consumer culture.

❖❖❖

In case I've confused matters with illustrations and excessive details, let me at this point add that the 1966 Chicago events are significant chiefly for making red-lining an issue of national significance. It had to happen somewhere, but for reasons entirely fortuitous, red-lining first became an issue in Chicago's western parts. What follows is the story of a decade-long struggle culminating in the 1977 Community Reinvestment Act and the formal ending of discrimination in mortgage-lending.

Direct action was at the core of the ten-year movement. One activist involved in the Chicago Freedom Movement was Saul Alinsky. He was one of many such activists in the late 1960s, but one with a knack for direct action.[13] Another was a woman named Gail Cincotta, who like Alinsky believed in direct action. She was capable of a nailing dead rat to the front doors of Chicago aldermen to persuade him to act. Alinsky was capable of gathering a dozen or so men, occupying all the urinals in

Part Two—The Deregulated Society

the men's room at O'Hare Airport, and staying there until his demand was addressed.

The problem they were protesting was the underlying cause of contract sales, namely, the inability of African Americans to obtain a bank mortgage. The response of local financial institutions was that they were doing no more than upholding traditional high standards in order to reduce risk. On the other side, so pressing were the direct approach of activists like Alinsky, Cincotta and others like them that they resulted in pressure on Congress to pass legislation.

The first such piece of legislation was the *1974 Equal Credit Opportunity Act* (ECOA), the name of which tells us that the 1968 Fair Housing Act had omitted including financial institutions, perhaps intentionally.[14] The 1974 law made it unlawful for any financial institution offering credit to discriminate on grounds of race or other identity categories, even when the applicant's income mainly derived from welfare assistance.

Such abstract reasoning was fine, but the real significance of the ECOA lay in its enforcement mechanism, called "Regulation B."[15] Failure to comply with Regulation B subjected a financial institution to civil liability for damages in individual or class action suits. Liability for punitive damages might be as much as $10,000 in individual actions and the lesser of $500,000 or 1 percent of the creditor's net worth in class actions. This gave teeth to the law and enabled it to bite. For the first time, the banks began to change.

Passage of ECOA also had the effect of encouraging more action at the grass roots level, where Cincotta was hard at work. The chief result was the 1975 Home Mortgage Disclosure Act (HMDA),[16] which quickly changed the terms of enforcement in such a way as to accommodate activists like Cincotta and the species of activism she represented. The purpose of HMDA and its Regulation C was to provide the public with adequate information demonstrating whether financial institutions were serving the credit needs of neighborhoods and communities in which they were located. The HMDA was a disclosure act and was part of a gathering movement for greater transparency in government. The fact that there was nothing substantive about the HMDA only underscored the growing significance of transparency as a political value.

That movement was then amplified by the passage of the aforementioned 1977 Community Reinvestment Act (CRA).[17] It directed regulated depository institutions to offer credit in all areas (neighborhoods)

11. Brown, Civil Rights and the End of the New Deal

in which they did business, meaning in red-lined neighborhoods as well as the other formerly color-coded neighborhoods. The banks howled at what they perceived to be a decline in vetting standards. For that reason they won their only concession: Congress agreed (section 802) that bank practices should be consistent with safe and sound operations. This made the law internally contradictory, for what the government wanted was to have the banks approve more loans that were sub-prime but also do so in a manner that was consistent with safe and sound operations, which they were not.

The new pressure to approve sub-prime loans was not the only problem that depository institutions had. The 1970s was beginning to be characterized by what economists called *stagflation*, or the inflation of prices, including interest rates, coupled with a stagnation of wages. For their part, savings & loan institutions were saddled with fixed-rate mortgages on which financial institutions earned 3 or 4 percent, while interest rates were rapidly climbing toward the double digits. What counted as "safe and sound conditions" was becoming a problem of monumental proportions.

Financial institutions did not want to be pushed further by a government whose interests were more about maintaining the peace than balancing the books. In respect to African American neighborhoods, the financial institutions were correct insofar as the government was trying to solve problems of discrimination in housing and credit without addressing other and related problems, like job discrimination. If the government paid as much attention to jobs as it did to housing, then African Americans would not be saddled with the problem of being chronically sub prime candidates for mortgages. But that consideration was beside the point that the government was only willing to take on housing problems.

So unfolded the 1970s, a forgotten but pivotal decade in United States history.[18]

❖ ❖ ❖

The 1977 Community Reinvestment Act did more than just enact change in the housing sector. It also called attention to the changing character of the Democratic Party. A decade earlier, the Party had pivoted in the direction of making African Americans its signature constituency but without ceasing to cater to the white unionized working class as its base constituency. Over the course of the 1970s African

Part Two—The Deregulated Society

Americans emerged as the core of a new base constituency of minorities. For the Party, the reversal was as significant as the shifts associated with the 1934 Housing Act had been.

The transition was initiated on television in Chicago at the 1968 Democratic convention, Mayor Daley's convention. It was signaled as underway in 1972 when Jesse Jackson unseated Mayor Daley as the head of the Illinois delegation. The Party's signature constituency ceased being one and became any self-identified minority that could secure five minutes on the microphone at the 1972 Party convention. The shift to identity politics was furthered with the victory of Jimmy Carter in the 1976 election, but it cannot be said that 1976 rang in a new era of Democratic victories. On the contrary, the Democrats would not again win the White House until 1992, a hiatus of twelve years.

The astute reader might sense that I attach enhanced significance to the legislative activities of the 1970s and wonder why that is the case. The reader is correct and the reasons should at least be indicated. I did not always agree with my one-time colleague Judith Stein about where she placed her emphases, but I did agree that the 1970s was a *pivotal* decade.[19] Charles Beard and the Progressive era were finally laid to rest, as was Franklin Roosevelt and the New Deal, and the Cold War policies that had worked wonders in Germany and Japan were now being considered in respect to China. But in looking at the decade, Professor Stein did not adequately perceive how changing financial practices would themselves prove pivotal. As a piece of legislation, the 1977 Community Redevelopment Act is as significant as the 1934 Housing Act. It is for the obvious reason that it opened the door for African Americans to participate in the consumer society. It also opened the way to another possibility, however, which was a more thorough revision of an early generation's financial regulations. I will pick up on that theme in Chapter 14, after first considering in more detail than I have here the nation's two political parties.

12

The 1970s: New Republicans and Old Democrats

In this book's first chapter I developed a rudimentary survey of the two great American political parties, taking them up to the 1950s. At that point in time, the Republicans won with Dwight D. Eisenhower, despite their candidate being the least of Republicans. The Democrats lost twice but knew they would win if their candidate was acceptable and the Republican candidate was, well, an authentic Republican. But then the civil rights movement turned everything upside-down, leaving the post–1968 Democrats in the difficult position of having to reconstruct their base before the 1972 election.[1]

The irony of that period was that in 1972 the party placed its fate in the hands of the relatively unknown George S. McGovern, who was charged with making new rules to make the Party more democratic, with a small "d." In doing this, McGovern grasped that the new rules he was making favored no candidate more than himself, and so he changed horses midstream and became the candidate of the party he was creating. A more sudden rise from obscurity to the top of a major political party was unknown in American political history.

Of all presidential elections of the preceding and succeeding twenty years, none was more significant that the 1972 election, for not only did the Democrats lose decisively, they also committed themselves to a new base of voters that would determine the Party's politics for the next twelve years. The keystone of the new arch of popular support was the African American community, or putting the situation more accurately, the African American communities (plural) of several American states. Though African Americans were well-positioned in cities like New York

Part Two—The Deregulated Society

and Chicago, still they comprised not much more than 11 percent of the national vote and so they had to be supplemented, and quickly.[2]

The prime candidate to supplement the African American vote was not a minority at all but rather a majority, namely, women. The problem, however, was that 1970s women were supposed to be united around the Equal Rights Amendment but were not. Urban feminists backed it solidly, but suburban women did not, and so when it failed to muster the state certifications to confirm it as an amendment to the constitution, the Democrats knew they were in trouble.

The alternative was to make up the difference with other minorities from among the numerous representatives that had spoken out until 3 a.m. on the day of George McGovern's nomination, but here a problem of a different sort arose. All of the other American minorities were small in number and difficult to concentrate and mobilize as voting blocks. Veterans, for example, were significant but were sprawled over the electoral map and so difficult to bring to focus. Jews were an excellent example of how things were supposed to work, concentrated as they were in several swing states and so having an influence in American electoral politics out of proportion to their raw numbers. The problem, however, was that they were already counted as basic to the Democratic Party.

That left the blue-collar unions, among which the UAW had been in the lead for twenty years. Here the first problem was that Walter Reuther was dead and though his successors were competent, they could not match Reuther for charisma, and so starting in 1972, the UAW paid its dues and put in an appearance but little more. Labor in the 1970s was a sagging source of support for the Democratic Party.

To say the Democrats nonetheless won the 1976 presidential election and did so with the remodeled base described above is to make a questionable claim. Yes, Jimmy Carter beat Gerald Ford, but Ford was a weak candidate throughout. True, Carter won handily, and he won Congress with ease, but if Democrats thought they had found a magic formula in their base, they were mistaken. They would find out how weak Carter really was when he ran against a strong Republican candidate in 1980.

If there was a lesson to be learned in 1980, the Democrats didn't learn it at all. Four years later they chose Jimmy Carter's vice president, Walter Mondale, to be their presidential candidate. Mondale was from Minnesota, Hubert Humphrey's home state, and he did bring that state home for the Democrats, but he brought home little else other than the

12. The 1970s: New Republicans and Old Democrats

predictable Washington, D.C. Choosing a woman as a running mate did Mondale little good.

Mondale's unsuccessful campaign was conducted against the backdrop of the Rev. Jesse Jackson's highly successful failure to win the Democratic Party's 1984 nomination. Jackson's bid was a little like Joe Robinson's campaign as vice-presidential nominee in the 1928 presidential election. Robinson won nothing, but his successful campaign in southern states contrasted sharply with Al Smith's failed campaign in northern states. That much carried a message to which Franklin D. Roosevelt paid close attention: only a northern Democrat could win the presidency, but the Northern Democrat could not do it without the vital help of a Southern Democrat in bringing home the so-called solid South.

The corresponding message in the 1980s was that only a white man could win the presidency, but to do so he needed the vital assistance of a black man, in this case the Rev. Jesse Jackson. The choice of Geraldine Ferraro as Mondale's running mate in 1984 had done nothing decisive for the ticket. Ferraro could not even bring home her home state of New York. But what if Mondale had chosen Jackson as a running mate? He certainly would not have done worse than with Ferraro, and Jackson's well-developed platform might even have brought home a couple of the more liberal Northern states. Short of that achievement, Jackson might still have brought home Illinois plus a couple of southern states. Mondale would likely still have lost the election, but he and the Democrats would have looked like better losers if a black running mate had brought home a few dozen electoral votes.

Besides race, a distinguishing feature of Jesse Jackson's campaign was his platform. Its major points identified every left liberal position of the future.[3] Even though African Americans were but a minority of 11 percent of the population, they could make a big difference if they were mobilized. Minimally they would enable the Democratic Party to lose better by looking better in the electoral contest at the center of the general election.

If mainstream establishment Democrats were fearful of Sen. Bernie Sanders in 2016 and 2020, they were terrified of Jesse Jackson in 1984. His kind of platform would have been familiar to American voters in pre–World War I elections, but since the prosecution of left liberal leaders under the 1918 Sedition Act, Americans had been taught to be unquestioning in respect to any program that suggested anything

Part Two—The Deregulated Society

social, with the term *socialized* turning into an all-purpose epithet. That the 1918 Sedition Act had been promoted and passed by a Democratic president did not make things any easier for the Democratic Party. From the 1919 Palmer raids to 1950s McCarthyism, Democrats were consistently exposed to charges of being "un–American" and therefore traitorous. Jackson's platform did not change this.

And so post–1984 Democrats found themselves in a quandary. Over twelve years and four national elections, they had lost two in which they had managed to win only a single state. They needed a new formula, and not just one that made them look respectable. They needed to win.

◈◈◈

The Republican Party in the period being apprised had been rebuilding through the 1970s but was no longer doing so after the 1980 election. The struggle in the 1970s was between the Party's centrists, led by Richard Nixon and Gerald Ford, and the Party's right wing, led by Ronald Reagan after the political demise of Barry Goldwater. The impeachment process against Nixon settled matters. The first really interesting intra-Party fight was between Ford and Reagan for the 1976 nomination. Ford won that fight, but the ghost of Barry Goldwater and the incarnation of Ronald Reagan eventually won over the Party.

A key moment in this evolution had to do with a 1971 memo written by future Supreme Court Justice Lewis Powell.[4] In the memo, which has since become legendary, Powell lamented the loss of a historic Republican culture in which businesspeople had legally incorporated and gained the high ground in American civilization. Powell was obviously regretting what might best be called the culture of the New Deal, or more specifically, the culture that authorized regulatory controls over every aspect of corporate business. Powell was especially irritated by the success of suburban upstart Ralph Nader in humbling a corporation like General Motors and the willingness of General Motors to bow to the pressure of such an ingrate as Nader.

The details of Powell's memo are not nearly as significant as its spirit, so I would address the latter and not the former.[5] Powell wanted and so urged his fellow Republicans to regain their rightful supremacy in this, *their* civilization, theirs because of its essential commercial character and all the social good that it did. Powell was angry at Nader for being ungrateful, but more widely it was clear he was angry not so much at poor people or African Americans or even the unionized blue-collar

12. The 1970s: New Republicans and Old Democrats

working class but rather at those supporters who had shown ingratitude for all the benefits that had been showered on them by the corporate civilization that General Motors had come to represent. Ralph Nader happened to be the latest exemplar of this upheaval, but Betty Friedan or any number of ungrateful, upper middle class college students would have qualified just as well.

Powell's memo struck a nerve, or at least it struck a nerve in the right places. Perhaps even more significant was the blow-out character of the 1972 election victory of Richard Nixon over George McGovern. The new confidence bred of victory on the field of battle led to the creation of the Heritage Foundation in 1973. Of all Republican think tanks established in the 1970s, this one merits all the attention it gets. Nonetheless, to understand it fully, we need to place it in context, or in its relation to similar events on the other side of the Atlantic Ocean.

The Heritage Foundation was founded with a close eye on Britain's *Centre for Policy Studies*, founded by Keith Joseph and Margaret Thatcher a year later. Both think tanks operated on similar premises: elected politicians were too compromised to be trusted to make policy. That vital function had therefore to be placed outside electoral politics in the hands of ideologically reliable experts in agencies beyond the sphere of electoral politics. Hence the Centre for Policy Studies and the Heritage Foundation.

The ideology was stated more clearly and emphatically in publications of the Centre for Policy Studies. Policies to be recommended had to adhere to the principles of free markets, the small state, low taxation, self-determination, responsibility, and national independence. Only after passing tests posed by those principles would policies be advocated by the Centre for Policy Studies.

The Heritage Foundation was not then or later so precise in its requirements, but this was likely because Margaret Thatcher was beginning to exert a strong influence in British conservatism and was not so demanding as Keith Joseph. Her counterpart, Ronald Reagan, was still far from Washington, D. C., and far from his rise to the top of the Republican Party in 1980, and so there was no mellowing influence on the Heritage Foundation in its earliest years.

The details of the reconstruction of the Republican Party in the 1970s are murky, but by looking at them through British eyes, we can more clearly see where they are going. With Gerald Ford still in the White House for two more years or more, political shifts in the

Part Two—The Deregulated Society

Republican Party were blurred in the United States. Clearly, however, the Party was on the path to becoming more conservative, more committed to the rule of big business, and eager to be rid of the allegiance to the New Deal that had corrupted Republicanism from Eisenhower through Nixon.

Whatever we say about these changes, they worked in the 1980 election. With Reagan as its nominee, the Republicans easily beat Jimmy Carter and more significantly achieved greater if not decisive power in Congress. Reagan repeated his victory in 1984, this time in a landslide victory that sent the Democratic Party into deep depression.

❖❖❖

Reagan's overwhelming 1984 re-election victory provoked some in the Democratic Party to believe that radical change was needed. But this time the change was going to take a riskier form and be more difficult to bring to the center of the party. The 1988 election promised a new beginning against a shakier Republican candidate in Vice President George H.W. Bush and his singularly unqualified vice presidential choice, Dan Quayle. The Democrats nominated Governor Michael Dukakis of Massachusetts, and he paired himself with Senator Lloyd Bentsen of Texas, making the election appear an easy victory for the Democrats. The rest of the story is well known. Dukakis failed at key moments, and the Republicans won the election.

Al From was a member of that small army of experts that Washington, D.C. is always awash with. The difference in From's case was that the praise was merited. At one time or another over the 14 years between 1971 and 1985, From held nearly every major administrative position on capitol hill for the Democrats.[6] He finally stepped back in 1985 and founded the Democratic Leadership Council (DLC), an organization he would head for the next two decades.[7] Two politicians he attracted to the DLC in its early years were Arkansas Governor Bill Clinton and Tennessee Senator Al Gore.

A common misconception about the DLC was that it simply adopted Republican principles and applied them to the Democratic Party. While true, such a brief description is also misleading in that it fails to capture the full array of work done by the DLC before Clinton's 1992 victory and over the next eight years. The DLC was at that time the key source of policy initiatives for the Clinton White House. Ideas such as a national service to replace the earlier draft, an earned income

12. The 1970s: New Republicans and Old Democrats

tax credit, charter schools, community policing, and welfare reform began with Al From before they became announced policy in the White House. Needless to say, the eventual repeal of Glass-Steagall was also a policy initiative coming from the DLC.

In many respects, the DLC was to the Democrats what the Heritage Foundation was to the Republican Party, but with one decisive difference that had to do with the principles adopted by both think tanks. The principles that underlay policy prescriptions coming out of the Heritage Foundation were authentically Republican principles. This was not the case with the Democratic Leadership Council. Instead, it let it be known that the Democratic Party no longer had any principles, that it could win elections by appealing directly to the interests of Republican constituencies and simply adding these to traditional Democratic constituencies.

Nowhere would the absurdity of this policy direction become more evident than in Great Britain, where Prime Minister Tony Blair adopted similar strategies and with great success. Big Business in Britain was happy with Blair, but so too were persons living in Council housing and dependent on government welfare. And so too were persons dependent on the National Health Service (NHS), who might imagine that the Conservative Party would terminate it but that Blair and the Labour Party would never do anything harmful to the NHS.

Amidst all the change of the 1970s and 1980s, the question emerges why the Democratic Party pivoted so radically from being a New Deal party to being an operation that opposed the New Deal. How do we explain it?

An initial approach to the question is to remind ourselves that the shift took place over a long period of time, perhaps 20 years, and that what is being characterized as a 180 degree turn is perhaps better characterized as a series of much smaller turns, each of only a few degrees. The problem with this response is that it both is and is not correct. It is perhaps correct for most Democratic operatives, but it does not describe the politics of Al From. From headed the House Democratic Caucus from 1980 to 1985 and so was in a good position to watch the Democrats hit bottom in a performance that matched their 1972 fiasco. When one considers that From founded the Democratic Leadership Council in 1985, it is likely that his experience at the center of House legislative affairs played some role.

Part Two—The Deregulated Society

But there is no proof of this, and so it is more likely that From is explicable only as a man of considerable political insight who was not afraid to draw radical conclusions about the character of American politics in the 1980s. Yet such an argument is more an admission of failure than an explanation. More likely, better can be done.

The better explanation of From is one that posits From as someone willing to confront difficult facts as well as someone who stands out in a party unwilling to confront the difficult fact that the New Deal was dead. Innumerable Democrats in the 1980s harbored a nostalgia for the New Deal and an inclination to devote their every waking thought to ways to revive it. From was the hyper-realist who recognized failure and recognized it fully after the 1984 election debacle. Copying the winning strategy in that election is a fairly obvious way to proceed, especially when the winning strategy returned victories in 49 of the 50 states.

Someone might have told From that his ideas, or idea in the singular, was all too simple, that he had better do a little more work. To that From might have replied that it was better to be simplistic, win the election, and then apply imagination to ways of governing, which is in fact what From did after 1992.

13

Depository Institutions and the Flowering of Bain Capital

Over the course of the 1970s, Republicans regained their confidence by dint of multiple rearrangements of corporate money that enabled owners rather than shareholders or managers to keep or regain control of it. For the most part, this rearranging of financial matters was a matter of keeping the money out of government regulated banks and putting it into arrangements independent of government regulation. Such arrangements were generally called *private equity*, and they worked perfectly for the owners insofar as they were beyond most government regulations. Venture capital funds emerged alongside vulture capital funds as well as funds with no capital at all but with the skill to borrow money on the basis of collateral they would seize and take private.

The core idea behind all such activity was that private was not public, meaning that money so held could not be regulated by public authorities like the Securities and Exchange Commission, the Federal Reserve Bank Board, or the Federal Reserve system of banks. The idea was not new, but its activation in the 1970s was.

One man positioned to understand what I am talking about was Richard Nixon's Treasury Secretary, William E. Simon. By 1978, Nixon and his vice-president were both past tense and Simon had had plenty of time to think about what it meant to be a private person. For him, privacy meant being able to do whatever one wanted, for whatever else the public sector was, it was filled with determinants on how one behaved. The public sector came with every manner of constraint and they took some of the joy out of being a businessman.

Part Two—The Deregulated Society

In 1978, Simon partnered with a tax accountant named Ray Chambers to form the Wesray Capital Corporation.[1] They borrowed money on the basis of Simon's name as well as the redefined assets of the company they would buy and take private. They used their considerable advantages to complete their purchase of the Gibson Greeting Card Company, a publicly traded firm. They then took the firm private, laid off excessive workers, and modernized equipment, all on credit. Then, no doubt taking some time to spread the word of what had been done, and at considerable profit, they took the company public again. Nearly all of this had been done on borrowed money (credit), and so the creditors had to be paid, but when the day's work was done, Simon and his partner walked away with a good deal of profit.[2]

Wesray demonstrated many things, but its most interesting effect was political and had to do with the logic of policy in United States constitutional arrangements. In their 1932 book, Adolf Berle and Gardiner Means assumed private property to be an inalienable right and so based their argument favoring regulation on the claim that the act of incorporation entailed the loss of precisely that right. Even if Henry Ford controlled a company named "Ford Motors," all of his actions were subject to regulation if half of the money that financed that company came from persons whose only reward was owning shares of the company.

Incorporation entailed the creation of a new public sector casually called *the stock market.* Just as Dutch share holders in ships sailing to the Spice Islands needed government regulation of ship captains to ensure that they didn't stop along the way back and sell part of the cargo to a pirate ship, so too shareholders in New York City needed oversight of the companies in which they owned shares to make certain they did not sell some of the proceeds of a Dakota copper mine to some pirate operation. They were absolutely right in this critically important argument.

Simon and Chambers assumed the same logic but reversed its direction. They took Gibson Greeting Cards private in order to restore the unalienable character of that piece of property. Of course, a few other presuppositions had to be in place, like the presence in the White House of a man who would not bog down the process in litigation. That was in fact the case with Jimmy Carter as well Ronald Reagan. The New Deal was dead not simply because a few leftist Democrats were sore about their 1968 experience in Chicago. The New Deal was dead because mainstream Democrats as well as former Democrats like Reagan were unwilling to defend it. But such feelings were no more than

13. Depository Institutions and the Flowering of Bain Capital

sentiment if no one acted on the feelings. Clever businessmen like William Simon were willing to stand the New Deal's legal logic on its head.

◈◈◈

Simon's operation was or a time unique, but not for long. In 1984, a small group of Boston investors led by Bill Bain and Mitt Romney founded Bain Capital. Bill Bain soon enough parted ways, leaving the company under the sole control of Romney, who found it convenient to continue with the name *Bain*. What Romney then did is the stuff of business school lore. He routinized his operation by modeling it on that of William E. Simon and his Wesray corporation, raising capital against the assets of prospective acquisitions, then buying them with the acquired capital, taking them private, laying off employees and otherwise modernizing the companies. At that point the son of the former CEO of the American Motors confronted a choice: either stay private and reap the benefits of having no regulation or file a new introductory public offer (IPO) and reemerge at significant immediate profit as a public company and return to life under the watchful gaze of the SEC. The choice was not always so cleanly arranged but having the choice at all was one of the distinguishing features of Bain Capital.

Where Wesray had stopped after two or three companies, Bain Capital continued to expand systematically in this fashion, acquiring such household corporate names as Staples, Burger King, Toys"R"Us, Dunkin' Donuts, and the like.[3] For a while in the first decade of this century it looked as though Boston had returned to the 1850s, when its banks were the wealthiest in the nation.[4]

As the number of companies so acquired accumulated, Romney saw fit to have Bain Capital change itself internally by ceasing to be a direct participant. Instead Bain Capital increasingly became a consulting firm, but one with its fingers always in the pie. Experienced Bain managers oversaw the activities of younger financiers, holding their hands at moments when they were required to jump and so teaching them how private equity worked from beginning to end. In doing this kind of thing in the last decade of the old century, Bain became the model for the private equity industry as a whole, so much so that the firm's history became required reading for students crowding into the nation's business schools.

Mitt Romney's tenure with the firm began to dissolve in 1999 when he left to run the Salt Lake Organizing Committee for the 2002 Winter

Part Two—The Deregulated Society

Olympics. Romney kept a finger in the pie for two additional years but finally negotiated a ten-year retirement agreement with Bain in 2002. Romney was the first and last CEO of Bain Capital. Since his departure, the company has been run by a management committee.[5]

Reviewing the history of leveraged and other buyouts since the 1980s gets us ahead of the story, however. It is preferable at this point that we step back and look at a different mirror to track the career of American money. That different mirror takes us to the nation's S&Ls, the subject of the 1980 Depository Institutions Deregulation and Monetary Control Act (DIDMCA).

❖ ❖ ❖

Private equity and even private equity funds were not new to the 1970s, but they returned with a vengeance in that decade, partly at least because of the development opportunity with college endowments and corporate pension funds. A characteristic feature of the latter was a felt need to keep the funds growing at a healthy rate. That was, after all, the reason money managers were hired in the first place. The funds had constantly to invest and do so where they could make the greatest profit. Venture capitalists soon enough discovered that pension funds were an excellent source of capital. While venture capitalists were making that discovery, another group called *money-brokers* was waking up to the same reality.

In those years, the chief characteristic of a money-broker was that he or she was not passive. To thrive, he or she had to make the connection between the languishing money pool and the investment opportunity in order to collect the commission fee, and so money brokers began to become very active at the end of the 1970s. The losers in all this were the nation's Mom-&-Pop banks, the S&Ls of the nation's Main Streets, for their savings accounts could not match the profits promised by the brokers.

And so Congress was compelled to rewrite the regulations that governed the nation's S&Ls in order to once again make them a secure place for ordinary Americans to keep their savings. I have not spoken of such regulations often in this book but have rather assumed them, starting in the first New Deal. But where the big investors of Wall Street banks had mixed feelings about regulation, the small savers of Main Street did not. They wanted the S&Ls to be regulated. That, after all, was where they kept the family's savings and hopes.

13. Depository Institutions and the Flowering of Bain Capital

The 1980 Depository Institutions Deregulation and Monetary Control Act came as something of a surprise.[6] It was the term *deregulation* that made everyone nervous, but to calm those nerves, Congress in its wisdom decided to increase FDIC insurance of demand accounts to $100,000, a large sum by any measure, but a comforting one for the Moms and Pops of the nation's Main Streets. The S&Ls were allowed to raise interest rates, invest in riskier ventures like condominium homes, furniture outlets, or fast food emporiums, and rake in greater profit to pay the higher interest rates the ban now offered. What could possible go wrong?

To understand what, we need only a little imagination and one or two examples. Anyone with the upstanding credentials and the right mix of assets could purchase an already existing S&L. In an existing climate of double-digit inflation, such a purchase was unlikely, however. It would only happen if the surrounding investment opportunity was favorable, and so such a purchase was a ready indicator of intention. S&L regulators (the Federal Home Loan Bank Board) should therefore have been on the alert, especially if one of their own was going to get into the business.

A clever financier might then offer a high interest rate to attract capital, at least enough to attract the attention of managers of pension funds and college endowments. With the money coming in, the financier might then advise the distant depositor to separate the money he or she was investing into $100,000 packets in order to be fully insured.

For any aspiring venture capitalist capable of reading the legislation, the newly defined situation presented a stunning opportunity to commit a piece of legally condoned fraud: buy a local bank, raise its interest rates, inform pension funds and endowments, draw in their money, and then connect with a developer who was capable to taking advantage of nearby opportunities to build condominiums, furniture stores, and fast-food restaurants for them to use as temporary offices. Then invest the money in risky ventures, win big if the investments worked but be fully covered by FDIC insurance if they failed.[7] All of this was done at no loss to the pension funds and possibly at considerable profit to the bank owner and the developer he or she had partnered with.

So much was theory for the men who bought the Empire Savings & Loan outside of Dallas, Texas, in 1981.[8] Opportunity was first recognized by an insider. Spencer H. Blain, Jr., was a bank regulator working out of the federal government's Little Rock office. He

Part Two—The Deregulated Society

resigned from the position, borrowed money and used it to purchase the Empire S&L, where he soon enough had himself declared the chief operating officer (CEO) charged with deciding where the bank's money would be lent.

All Blain needed was a developer, and he soon enough had one in the person of an illiterate housepainter named Danny Faulkner.[9] The bank financed Faulkner, who in turn staked-out lots around a staked-out golf course, both bordering on Lake Ray Hubbard. An accomplished pilot as well as housepainter, the illiterate Faulkner then took prospective buyers on helicopter tours to view their staked-out property from the air. He also laid the foundations for condominium buildings along Rt I-30, generously waiving the usual requirements for persons who longed for a home but were otherwise NINJA candidates (No Income, No Job, No Anything). Faulkner would make a call to nearby Empire Savings to smooth the way for a quick approval. He had a friend there.

It all worked well enough until understaffed federal authorities discovered fraud at the Mesquite bank, which in its case amounted to the bank's not being able to pass a stress test related to the quality of its loans to figures like Danny Faulkner and the persons who were granted the NINJA home mortgages. The justification for the test was not some whim on the part of the government. It was rather the federal obligation, assigned to the Home Loan Bank Board, to protect the bank's other customers, which in the Mesquite case were in on the scam from the outset because of the FDIC coverage. Left holding many different bags was the federal government.

The Mesquite case was only one of many in the 1980s saga called "the savings and loan crisis" or for short, "the S&L Crisis." It pays to understand the logic of this crisis.

❖ ❖ ❖

One way to approach the matter was to declare the nation's savings associations insolvent and end the government guaranteed lending programs created in the 1934 Housing Act. No more homes for the blue-collar working class. Back to those overcrowded Brooklyn tenements. But the Carter administration could not bear to do such a thing. It still had enough loyalty to the New Deal to do what it could to save one of its marquis programs. Therefore, the Carter administration signed off on the 1980 Depository Institutions Act. It would loosen the

13. Depository Institutions and the Flowering of Bain Capital

tight controls of the New Deal era and increase the FDIC insurance so that savings banks could do a more profitable business than they could with those low-profit home mortgages.

It is difficult to grasp on what grounds the federal government thought the hometown thrifts would stay in the home mortgage business. It had to be an act of faith on the part of Congress and the Carter administration. Most banks would not do what the Empire Savings Association had done when it was bought by Spencer Blain. Most banks would continue to give out loans to worthy home buyers and maintain their reserves by means of high interest paid to pension funds and endowments who were parking their money with those banks. But the entire operation was internally contradictory. The nation's S&Ls had to find (or be given) legally condoned ways to earn more money.

Naively or not, the Reagan administration expanded the DIDMCA policy by signing off on the 1982 Garn-St. Germain law.[10] It authorized banks to offer flexible mortgage rates as another way to increase their profits. This made sense from the banks' point of view but not from the perspective of the blue-collar worker. The New Deal idea of a fixed interest rate with a thirty-year duration was the foundation of the notion that blue-collar workers could be induced to become lifetime savers. On the assumption that his assembly line job would last for at least 30 years, he was in effect being put into a straitjacket for 30 years but rewarded at the end with a home that he could sell to finance his retirement.

Garn-St. Germain amounted to one more recognition that the New Deal formula was no longer viable. A flexible interest rate (ARMs) meant that the home buyer might get an artificially low "teaser" rate at the outset, only to see it rise significantly after a number of years, usually three or five. Hence, the buyer, if he or she was clever, would put his home up for sale after four years, profit from the sale, pay off the mortgage, and start all over again. Or if the buyer were not clever, he or she would get hit with the higher rate, lose his or her job, and experience the bank foreclosing on his or her home. In other words, time had run out on the New Deal. Its protections for the working class were no longer working.

Rightly understood, Garn-St. Germain assumed a different kind of homeowner than the one assumed by the 1934 Housing Act. The earlier act assumed a steady worker, skilled perhaps but over time more

Part Two—The Deregulated Society

likely to be deskilled or unskilled and so committed to the boredom of a lifetime of repetitive motions on a Ford or GM assembly line. A further assumption in 1934 was that the productive process had ceased to be seasonal and that a government committed to straitening out inclinations toward depression and inflation existed, hence providing an external guarantee that the blue-collar worker would be steadily employed.

Not so the 1982 Garn-St. Germain Act.[11] It did not so much dismiss the continuing possibility of steady assembly line work as cease to take it for granted. Fixed exchange rates continued to be available, but with stories being told of companies closing and moving their production lines to the Guangdong Province in China, no one was so confident of a 30 year job doing repetitive work on a classic assembly line. The more likely case was that of a worker losing his job on an assembly line and finding work elsewhere in some service job, ideally with the local or state government but if not then with a retail store such as a supermarket. With the reduction in wages such a change entailed, it was likely that the woman of the house also took a job, entailing the necessity of purchasing a second car.

All of the latter being the case, an adjustable interest rate on a home mortgage was attractive. It lowered costs significantly for the first few years and could be made into a positive benefit if the homeowner planned to sell after five years and buy a home ten miles further out on the interstate and with a fresh start and with a new adjustable-rate mortgage.

None of the above happened in a moment or to everyone at the same time, but what did happen across the nation and on the front pages of newspapers was the Savings & Loan Crisis, and it as much as any local factory closing brought the overall crisis of consumer society into living rooms and to kitchen tables across the United States. And then, as if there wasn't enough evidence of the sea-change that was happening, the figure of Charles Keating appeared, and so the crisis associated with his name began to unfold.

❖❖❖

Charles Keating led two related but separate lives. In Arizona he was the chairman and controlling stock owner of a development firm called the American Continental Corporation, which at the end of the 1980s was constantly involved in building luxury resorts and

13. Depository Institutions and the Flowering of Bain Capital

single-family homes targeted to military retirees. In California, on the other hand, Keating was the owner of the placid Lincoln Savings Association in San Diego. Because they both belonged to Charles Keating, the left hand certainly knew what the right hand was doing, but most everyone else including federal regulators did not.

When in 1988 American Continental found itself in financial difficulties, Keating had a solution. He created high yield corporate bonds in the American Continental's name to be sold by his managers to savers in possession of large savings accounts at Lincoln Savings. In keeping with DIDMCA, Lincoln certificates worth $100,000 each were fully insured by he FDIC. Not so the higher yielding corporate bonds of American Continental, however. But Lincoln's clients were kept in the dark about the risk they were taking on. That little piece of information made the Keating operation questionable and gave the government an opening to intervene. The real problem, however, was that Charles Keating was on both ends of the transaction.

The debacle at Lincoln was similar in some respects to the one at Empire Savings Association of Mesquite, Texas, but not entirely. The difference was that the depositors at Mesquite remained protected when their money was squandered on questionable development projects. The loser at Mesquite was the FDIC. With the Lincoln Savings and Loan, the story was different, with the loser being not the FDIC but rather the bank's customers.

From our point of view, the significance of the story has to do with the fundamentals of American consumer society, the most significant of which had to do with regulation. The entire 1930s and 1950s operation was conducted within the rules of existing government agencies, either federal or state. Home mortgages at rates fixed for thirty years were sold to Fannie Mae which in turn sold them to investors to raise money to plow back into the mortgage market. There was no point in the chain of transactions where anyone could lose.

Such was not the case with the supposedly deregulated markets of the 1980s. The investors were no longer reliably identified as ordinary folks entrusting their life savings to the local and familiar S&L on Main Street. They were pension or endowment plans or in the case of the Lincoln Savings & Loan, retirees were willing to consider the options and put their money at risk with corporate bonds. At no time was the motive of the 1980s programs to settle a blue-collar assembly-line worker into a situation that would yield an owned home that could be used

Part Two—The Deregulated Society

as a retirement fund. Everyone involved in 1980s practices was a risk taker. The difference was that some were better situated and so better informed than others.

At this point in a developing argument, I am not moralizing about any of the participants. It is easy to condemn Charles Keating and feel sympathy for Lincoln savers. I am doing neither because they were all risk-takers, the only difference being that Keating was better situated, meaning that he had better knowledge of happenings. Federal authorities were in both cases on the outside looking in, but in the 1950s they were looking at programs constructed with tight internal controls. Where there was corruption in the 1950s was in the racial aspects of federal programs. The corruption of the 1980s was not in the least racial but was rather entirely financial.

Finally, the programs of the 1950s and 1980s differed in that federal officials themselves were corrupted, Spencer H. Blain, Jr., in the Mesquite, Texas, case and several United States senators led by Dennis DeConcini and Alan Cranston in the Lincoln Savings & Loan case.

14.

The Privatized Mortgage Industry of the 2000s

The event that provoked the repeal of Glass-Steagall was the merger of the Citibank with Travelers Insurance, producing *Citigroup*, familiar to all of us from its red umbrella logo, inherited from Travelers. The legislation that brought about the repeal of Glass-Steagall is better known by the names of its authors, hence as Gramm-Leach-Bliley.[1] But of these three names, only one was of decisive importance, namely that of Senator Phil Gramm, Republican of Texas. Gramm was a charming professional economist with an ideological streak that did not seem likely in his otherwise friendly demeanor.

Gramm subscribed to the 18th century vision of the state as an aristocratic parasite fattening itself at the expense of commoners, or in American parlance, ordinary folks.[2] Gramm envisioned a realm of popular liberty in which ordinary Americans trucked-and-bartered their goods and services with complete freedom. This vision, conventionally assigned to Adam Smith, should not be underrated. It was and is the gospel of a worldly religion that sends its followers into ecstasies of joy and emboldens them to witness for their faith by acting to strip the state of its every hold on the economic lives of commoners. Gramm was a preacher leading his flock into the promised land, and Gramm-Leach-Bliley was a giant step forward on this worldly pilgrimage.

Congressman Jim Leach co-sponsored the bill but was as different from Phil Gramm as day was from night. He was a Republican elected in an increasingly Democratic district because he was an affable and well-rounded person who had not been captured by any narrow view

Part Two—The Deregulated Society

of deregulating the economy for the sake of maximizing liberty. Leach was the kind of sponsor who gave Democrats confidence that the repeal of Glass-Steagall was not an unmitigated descent into economic bedlam.[3]

Paying sole attention to the named authors of the Financial Services Modernization Act of 1999, the official name of Gramm-Leach-Bliley, is a mistake, however. The ultimate authors of the bill and legislation were the makers and shakers of Wall Street as well as their lobbyists in the nation's capital. Occasionally we are given a peek into this world, usually when one of its players turns apostate in order to save his immortal soul. In January 2012 Bill Moyers (of television fame) interviewed John Reed, the former CEO of Citibank and Citigroup.[4] That moment, in the judgment of this writer, is the one we are seeking.

Reed argued that animal exuberance had taken over Wall Street in the 1990s and altered the way everyone on the Street saw themselves and the world. Reed of course conveniently omitted that he was one of them, but it was Reed who was submitting to the interview and so it might be expected that he would spend some of his capital burnishing his tarnished reputation. Reed's partner in an act that was technically a crime was Sandy Weill, who in Reed's opinion dedicated his entire being to accumulating money.[5] Reed of course did not. He depicted himself as the duped junior partner of a master of financial malfeasance.

The deeper basis of the actions of Reed and Weill was the collapse of the original popular understanding of Glass-Steagall, or rather its spirit of protecting Main Street from Wall Street, of protecting commoners from financial predators. That spirit had been carried forward by Frank Capra in films like *Mr. Smith Goes to Washington* as well as *It's a Wonderful Life*, films not understood first time round but destined to become iconic. Glass-Steagall was remarkably simple: if you have a tiger in your zoo, don't open the cage door to see how it will behave in freedom. It's not worth the risk. Sandy Weill was the tiger, I guess, and Reed the fool who opened the cage door. There were other candidates for the appointed roles as well, but they are the main ones.

Nonetheless, it is a mistake to see collective actors like the Republican Party as the only ones wearing the black hats. Indeed, to assert that

14. The Privatized Mortgage Industry of the 2000s

the Democratic Party of Bill Clinton was every bit as complicit as the Republicans is to understate the case against that party. After Clinton's successful impeachment defense, the Democrats were eager to be the party receiving credit for "getting real." Repealing Glass-Steagall would thoroughly overshadow Clinton's dealings with Monika Lewinski, and so by 1999 the party held a winning hand with the winning card.

On the Washington side of the deal, and in the neoliberal Clinton administration, the key player was Treasury secretary Robert E. Rubin, who had previously spent a quarter century at Goldman, Sachs and was a man without a charitable bone in his body.[6] By the late 1990s Rubin had the reputation of being the leading neo liberal in what was by any measure already a neo liberal Democratic administration. Rubin was in favor of drawing every conceivable activity into a profit-making category.[7]

We need also to understand the background to Citigroup's activities. By 1999, S&Ls no longer thought of themselves as primarily in the home-mortgage business. Dispensing home mortgages had become a front behind which the hunt for more profitable investments was on. Innumerable S&Ls had become miniature investment banks, putting insured money into high-risk ventures like building condominiums and selling their units to NINJA applicants, politely called sub-prime.[8] Selling or granting mortgages was a line of activity that post–DIDMCA S&Ls maintained mainly as a front.[9]

To grasp what was going on, imagine the difference between a pharmacist and a drug dealer. The pharmacist knows that the pills he or she is dispensing are dangerous because addictive and so expects them to be prescribed only by an authority whose certification may be suspended by the state. I am of course speaking of a medical doctor, or MD.

The drug dealer knows equally well that the pills or shots he or she is dispensing without state-certified authority are dangerous and addictive. Nonetheless, he or she finds such information good reason for lowering the introductory price so that he can create the market before raising the price.

The driving force behind the new economy was not that of the pharmacist but rather that of the drug dealer. Reed knew this at the time and so was happy to enter into a relation with Weill. Their bet was that they would get certified by the state, which was a different way of saying that Glass-Steagall's proscription on such a relation would be voided.

Part Two—The Deregulated Society

To succeed, Citigroup would have to convert the retail operations of Mom & Pop S&Ls into wholesale operations more appropriate to Wall Street. The model commercial bank—in the days immediately after the repeal of Glass-Steagall, that was Citigroup—set about making a profit by buying mortgages, assembling them into bundles, and marketing them on a wholesale market of its creation. Such bundles were called collateralized-debt-obligations (CDOs) or mortgage-backed securities (MBSs), and they were meant to be sold to any organization with a great deal of money wanting a low-risk investment with decent profits. The operation contrasted with the ever popular *Titanic* model by having internal security. Failure for any individual mortgage was not like hitting an iceberg. A small leak would be sprung, one that was easily plugged, but at no time would the proverbial ship ever experience a tear too big for the crew to manage.

As with so many financial products, this one also depended on the purchaser's knowledge of a now rosy past. Mortgages granted in the 1950s were fixed-rate, thirty-year loans to conventional laborers with steady work on assembly lines in Los Angeles and Oakland, Birmingham and Atlanta, as well as Detroit, Akron, Toledo, Cleveland, and Pittsburgh. But this once real age had passed, and so knowledge of it had mutated into phantasy. Mortgages granted in the 1990s were often adjustable rate and were given to unconventional laborers who had seen their "steady" jobs exported to China and Mexico and were now working multiple less steady jobs in shopping malls. They were not bad people, but so unsteady were they that it became convention to eschew asking them for documentation as proof of their trustworthiness. Knowledge of this new softness of the working class was deep in the 1990s, but only for the financial elites. It had not yet made its way into popular literature.

Wall Street banks like Citigroup not only had this knowledge. They also had an interest in its *deniability*. They therefore abandoned that intersection where the rubber meets the road: the actual marketing of individual mortgages. They instead farmed this operation out to mortgage brokers. These were middlemen who had no vital stake in the viability of the mortgages they granted because they could immediately sell them to the Wall Street banks that would be bundling them for the wholesale market.

◆◆◆

14. The Privatized Mortgage Industry of the 2000s

The best-known such mortgage broker was Angelo Mozilo's *Countrywide Financial*, although *New Century Financial* was just as large.[10] Both companies were recent additions to the generic category *alternative financial services*. That however is a controversial claim that warrants being examined.

Traditionally, the category *alternative financial services* is reserved for operations like payday loans, check-cashing, money-transmission, and instant automobile insurance. Such services are conventionally located in sections of cities that are poor as well as minority, traditionally mainly in African American neighborhoods but more recently and increasingly in Hispanic neighborhoods. The persons being dealt with are unaccustomed to conventional banking services because they have not used them. They are distrustful as well, and so a service that charges a high rate but gives back instant performance is preferred.[11]

Why would mortgage brokers fall into the generic category of alternative financial services? The response is for the most part consequentialist: as a matter of statistical fact, the persons they are negotiating with for home mortgages are less than prime candidates, which in the parlance of the industry is to say that they are "sub-prime." This characteristic is in comparison with persons being dealt with by conventional banks, who are "prime" and know they are before they come through the door.

The loans were likely to be of the NINJA variety for the start. The latter are of two varieties: liars' loans and no-doc loans. The former indicates that the applicant is being questioned and compelled to tell lies, which only hold up because they are not documented. The latter indicate that the manager already knows that the applicant has no income, no job, no anything and so does not ask questions in the first place. It all gets complicated for no particularly good reason and so it is best to lump such loans together as NINJA.

The attraction of NINJA loans is that they are less expensive—*much* less expensive—to process. For that reason, either the original sponsoring bank is paying a lower commission, or the broker is earning a disproportionately greater commission or fee for managing this introductory process.

Why would presumably respectable banks like J.P. Morgan, Citibank, or Bank of America want to purchase such suspect mortgages? The answer has to do with supply and demand in the turn of the century

Part Two—The Deregulated Society

mortgage market. The banks could sell MBSs or CDOs at great profit *if* they had the raw material out of which to assemble them, but very often—indeed, *always*—the raw material was in short supply. The easy way to get the needed supply was for Citibank to ask no questions and simply take what Countrywide or one of the other alternative services had on offer.

The more basic question is whether the banks knew what they were doing. Of course, they did, but by not asking questions, Wall Street banks created *deniability* for themselves. At any moment in the market's development between 2000 and 2007 the Wall Street banks could have vetted their cull and discovered that it did not meet the expected standard of generally prime mortgages. Had they been culled, a percentage of sub prime mortgages could have been allowed into the mortgage backed securities because the failure of ten or fifteen percent of the total would not have toppled the MBS in question. What few outsiders suspected was that the center-of-gravity lay with the sub-prime mortgages, which may have been as much as sixty to seventy percent of the total, and the banks were willfully ignorant of what they had created.

A comparative example might help the reader to appreciate what was being done. The University of Phoenix does no vetting of applicants for its degree programs. Assuming the admission requirements are legitimate and are enforced (questionable at best), the university is guaranteed to make a profit solely from students who (predictably) do not complete program requirements. In the unlikely case of unqualified students who are determined to complete the requirements, they will need remediation that is not available, or if it is available, it is at the instructor's expense. Alternatively, instructors apply no rigor to requirements and so-called students hire surrogates to do the required work. By whatever route taken, a degree from the University of Phoenix is worth very little, unless the so-called university invests in lobbying to pressure the state to accept the credentialing of its so-called students. Then the student is a winner but the state a loser.

Back to the banks, where a second expectation came into play. The banks had insured their MBSs by purchasing from the American International Group (AIG) a product called a swap. *Swaps*, specifically credit default swaps, were derivatives in which the seller of the swap agrees to pay the buyer of the swap the principle and interest of a loan that has

14. The Privatized Mortgage Industry of the 2000s

been defaulted. In practice, a credit default swap is an insurance policy that pays in the case of default.

The problem in the case of AIG was that it did not have the reserves to pay all its swaps when the home-mortgage market collapsed in 2008. Having less than the required minimum is one species of insurance fraud. AIG would normally be tagged for this, but in fact it was following a growing practice in American financial arrangements of risking more than it could afford to cover.

A bank makes a profit by dint of two probabilities. The first is that not all its depositors will arrive on the same day and demand a return of all the money they have entrusted to the bank. The second is that all borrowers will not use all their credit on the same day, thus posing a stress-test that the bank cannot handle. The first is more significant than the second, but the second does count and should be noted. In the unlikely case that a bank's clients do all arrive on the same day and demand all their money, the bank manager is also covered by funds at other banks channeled through the Federal Reserve bank.

Increasingly American financial institutions were risking more than the statistical models allowed. A case in point was a California S&L named *IndyMac*. The fact that it failed was less interesting than the timing of its failure. *IndyMac's* failure to pass a stress-test was covered up by a bank inspector named Darrel W. Dochow, who dated the failure later than it actually was, giving the bank a grace period in which to make up for its laxness. Dochow's method is familiar to all of us: my algebra homework has to be turned in by the beginning of class at 11:05 a.m. on Monday. I'm a day late but beg the teacher give me a break and she does, letting me get it in by the same time one day later. It might all work out, but what's been done is unfair to the other students, who may have sacrificed in some unknown way to get their homework in at 11:05 a.m. Monday.

Dochow's act was much worse than the teacher who gave one tardy student a break. Dochow imposed an unnecessary risk on everyone by ignoring the bank's failure, whereas the teacher's action imposed no such risk. One might argue that Dochow was imposing no such added risk, that it was all "red-tape" to begin with and that banks should better operate on a *laissez-faire* model with no Darrel Dochow's to contend with, but such attitudes carried to the extreme take the tension out of society and cause everything to slump into a failing mode.

❖ ❖ ❖

Part Two—The Deregulated Society

The regulatory agency that Darrel W. Dochow worked for was the Office of Thrift Supervision (OTS), the successor fifteen years earlier to the then beleaguered Federal Home Loan Bank Board (FHLBB). The OTS was initiated because the same Dochow had failed to regulate Charles Keating's Lincoln Savings & Loan. Dochow was removed from his position but not from his job. Instead of being fired, he was demoted and reassigned from Washington, D.C., to his former position in Seattle. From that position, he proceeded to work his way back up the chain to become the lead OTS regulator for southern California. He was back at the place where his mischief started.

Even after the IndyMac scandal, Dochow was removed from his position but again, he was not fired or jailed. He was instead allowed to retire with a full pension, which he promptly did.[12] When asked about the latest of his remarkable string of failures, Dochow pleaded that he could not speak about such matters in public due to the risk of harming third parties, meaning apparently his superiors in the OTS or FHLBB. Darrel W. Dochow then passed away without ever explaining why he had behaved as he did.

The longtime soft-peddling of Dochow's "errors" is indicative of a more widespread culture in the regulatory realm, one that has been described cogently by a former regulator, William K. Black.[13] One of the Black's claims was that above and beyond the misdeeds of regulators, bank directors are seldom removed from their positions because it is known that their replacements will most likely expose their wrong doings. Put the other way round, miscreant bank directors are kept in their positions because it is known that they will not further expose wrongdoing. They are treated in approximately the same manner as Darrel W. Dochow was.

But in fact, Black argues, they are law breakers. They were in constant violation of the *Prompt Corrective Action Law*, which required bank officials to take corrective action early before a problem got out of hand.[14]

15

From Brooksley Born to Sarbanes-Oxley

A different example of deregulation, seemingly unrelated to the material in the previous chapter, concerned the marketing of over-the-counter (OTC) derivatives, precisely what mortgage backed securities (MBS) were. An instance of the latter had to do with the experience of Brooksley Born, head of the Commodities Futures Trading Commission (CFTC) from 1996 to 1999. Ms. Born was a competent regulator whose prior career was as a securities attorney in California.

Brooksley Born supported the pro-business orientation of the Clinton administration, but devoid of the ideology that fueled politicians like Phil Gramm, she firmly believed in the necessity of regulating business activities and thought furthermore that OTC derivatives fell under her aegis.

Born had earlier been considered for attorney general but was passed over by President Clinton, who is said to have found her boring.[1] Born was then named head of the CFTC, most likely a consolation prize, but she took the position with no hint of bitterness at not having been named attorney general.

Born's positive attitude may have been shaped by her expansive interpretation of her remit. A commodities future is conventionally an agricultural product that is sold today at an agreed upon price but for delivery tomorrow (or sometime in the future), at the originally agreed upon price. The value of such a contract is that is brings stability to the lives of both parties, the baker who wants to know today what he will have to pay for flour tomorrow and the farmer who knows now what he will receive for a crop not yet planted. The Commodities Futures Trading Commission was the regulator for such transactions.

There was nothing problematic with these arrangements as long as the insurer adhered to the basic rule of having always enough reserve money on hand to cover the range of likely mishaps. How to guarantee that this was the case was the problem Congress wanted addressed. The question, however, was the degree to which any CFTC administrator would be supported by the president if (or when) push came to shove when the expected problems arose.

Opposed to Brooksley Born were a number of persons who for their own reasons thought differently. One was Alan Greenspan, head of the Federal Reserve, and thus a figure coming at the problems of business with the different perspective of a libertarian. In other words, Greenspan was an ideologue who disagreed with the regulations he was sworn to uphold. That Greenspan was a contradiction in terms went without saying. How he would work out the contradiction in practice was an open question.

Secondly there was Robert E. Rubin, Clinton's secretary of the treasury, who had made his way up the corporate ladder entirely within Goldman, Sachs.[2] Rubin, whom we met in the previous chapter, was less ideologue than cut throat deal-maker who took the rules of the market to be impediments to getting more quickly to his goal. Finally there was Larry Summers, Rubin's acolyte and future successor and every bit as much the free marketer as Rubin was.

I would here pause for a moment's reflection on the convergence of forces Brooksley Born was confronting. Since the 18th century at least, the intellectual construct of economics has been rearranged to portray work as a natural activity and every activity that disturbs it as an unnatural and unjustified aberration. Adam Smith was the originator of this point of view, or if not the originator, certainly the popularizer.

The aforementioned opinion was often held by thinkers, academic or not, but seldom by policy makers, and almost never by several key policy-makers simultaneously, which happened to be the situation when Brooksley Born confronted Greenspan, Rubin, and Summers as well as Clinton in the White House and Gramm in the Senate. I hesitate to use the shopworn metaphor of the perfect storm, but in the guise of a well dressed Washington policy clique, that was exactly what Brooksley Born confronted during her tenure. The best advice for her would have been to submit or, short of such an unconscionable action, to resign with dignity and return to California. Brooksley Born chose neither alternative but rather opted to stay the course and suffer the

15. From Brooksley Born to Sarbanes-Oxley

consequences. The balance of this chapter tells the story of that metaphorically suicidal course.

◈ ◈ ◈

As high commissioner of the Commodities Futures Trading Commission, Born reported directly to the president and not to the head of the Federal Reserve or to the Secretary of the Treasury. Hence, Born did not report to Greenspan or Rubin, and unless the president made the unusual move of cutting her off at the outset, she was free to initiate moves that Greenspan and Rubin might be opposed to, like regulating OTC derivatives. This much Born was likely to do in commencement addresses or in speeches she made to luncheons held by corporate groups meeting in Washington. She would also do so in testimony to Congress. The question at all times would be whether she was generating support that would materialize in Congress.

Born did, starting with such activities with her testimony to the Senate Agriculture Committee of February 11, 1997.[3] In her opening statement, Born asked the Senate to reconfirm the CFTC's power to clearly and unambiguously prohibit all fraud in futures transactions and to confirm that those involved with questionable, off-exchange futures contracts and option contracts be found liable if they failed to register with the CFTC. She further asked the Senate to clarify the Commission's authority to bring civil enforcement proceedings for violations of the felony provisions of the act and to prohibit courts from assessing costs for or against the Commission in any proceeding brought under the act.

Of even greater significance, Born telegraphed her expectation that she expected a fight by making several similar public addresses over the next three months. On March 13, 1997, Born delivered remarks, entitled "The Dangers of Deregulation," to the Futures Industries Association. She made similar remarks on March 31 to a different professional group. Clearly Born was mounting a campaign to influence Congress to move in the direction of greater regulation of OTC derivatives.

Treasury Secretary Rubin was not caught off guard. He early understood what was happening and so called a late April 1998 meeting of the President's Working Group at the Treasury Department. Rubin invited Greenspan and Summers to attend and Born as well. Rubin and his backers were quick to get to the point. For them, Brooksley Born did not have the authority to dictate the terms of regulation and, in any case,

Part Two—The Deregulated Society

what she was doing was misguided because the OTC derivatives market was working well and generating immense profits. To publicly question its activities at this point in time would be disruptive to a significant market. She had to give it up or be stopped.

Outnumbered three to one by men who outranked her in every way, the lady proved to be not for turning. She insisted that she reported directly to the president and not to Secretary Rubin and that she very well understood how not to upset markets. As to the question of her authority, the very fact of the meeting being held indicated that she must have had such authority, else the meeting made no sense. The meeting ended courteously but with nothing resolved.

Born went on to deliver remarks supportive of added regulatory authority. In March, she addressed the Futures Industry Trading Commission's annual conference in Boca Raton, Florida.[4] Later she addressed a group called *Women in Housing and Finance* and in case that reaffirmation of her position was not clear, again on May 21 to the New York City and State bar associations.

Push came to shove at the morning of May 7, 1998, when Born authorized the publication of a concept release addressing her issues. A *concept release* is bureaucratese for a shot over the bow warning that action is imminent. But in her customary fashion, Brooksley Born may have had a fist of steel but was still a lady who preferred to wear a velvet glove. She pulled her punches and accorded equal time in every phase to the other side. Given who was on the other side and the multiplier by which they outnumbered her, this turned out to be a strategic mistake.

On May 7, 1998, Treasury Secretary Rubin responded with a letter made public. Also courteous, Secretary Rubin nonetheless did not mince words. His message was clear: *if it ain't broke, don't fix it.* The OTC derivatives market was not even close to being broke. It was working so well that it behooved Congress not only to dismiss Born's suggestions but also to make certain that the market was not upset by her misconceived notions of regulation.

May 7, 1998, came to an end as the day when the regulatory war became open. What followed was more or less a primer in Washington politics: play to win, but if it is impossible to win, then hold off to a day when the chances are better. Winning entails having committee support and then having a skilled point guard to lead legislation from committee to floor and on to the president's desk. Short of having these elements together, think twice before starting.

15. From Brooksley Born to Sarbanes-Oxley

Born may have reported directly to the president, but her president was a neo liberal who subscribed to freer and more profitable markets and had probably appointed Born to her post on gender grounds. It was Rubin, not Born, who had Clinton's ear. Clinton did not intervene, and his silence spoke volumes.

In respect to committee and floor fights, there is no evidence that Rubin crossed party lines, but it quickly became clear that he had Republican support, and moreover the support of Senator Phil Gramm of Texas, not only a fanatical deregulator but also a skilled political operative. While Democrats covered themselves by making statements for the *Congressional Record*, Republicans worked the crowd and accumulated the votes. It should have been clear early-on that Born and her position had little chance of succeeding.

And so it went through the fall of 1998, a period in which Senator Gramm reached the peak of his career as a Senate leader. Hearings were held and Gramm made it perfectly clear that he opposed all regulation of OTC derivatives. Moreover, as the legislation proceeded, it became clear that Born would not only lose but that her office as commissioner of the CFTC might even be shorn of its other powers. The point, it seemed, was not just to defeat her proposals but also to thoroughly humiliate the lady.

In Washington politics of the time, matters seldom got as personal as this fight did. Even across party lines, Republicans and Democrats tend to pull their punches. This fight was one of the rare occasions they didn't, and without proof, it would seem that an element of sexism was involved. Born had not deferred to the three men she met with—Rubin, Greenspan, and Summers in April 1997—and she may at that moment have crossed her Rubicon. To say she should have seen the writing on the wall and collected allies is easy enough, but Born might not have been able to so act. There were not that many Democratic women in positions of power in the late 1990s, and so Born may not have been able to gather a team of allies. In any case, Born resigned from the CFTC on June 1, 1999.

The result a year later was the Commodities Futures Modernization Act of 2000, which formalized the exemption of OTC derivatives from regulation as futures or securities.[5] The bill was signed with pleasure by President Clinton, indicating that he had stayed on the sidelines of the dispute between Born and Rubin because Rubin did not want him intervening. Rubin had little cause for concern.

Part Two—The Deregulated Society

In the midst of the painful process of defeating and humiliating Brooksley Born, the press arrived to put the finishing flourishes on Robert Rubin's decisive victory. While he was wrapping up the conflict with Born, Rubin had entered the final stages of another deregulatory effort, the legislation to repeal Glass-Steagall. Here the message of the era was crystal clear, for while the bill to repeal Glass-Steagall was named after Republican Senator Phil Gramm, *Time* magazine put pictures of Summers, Rubin, and Greenspan on its cover and called them the "Committee to Save the World."

❖❖❖

The years around the turn of the century were the Golden Age of deregulation, but what was exposed in the 2001 Enron scandal was shocking even to the most hardened operators on Wall Street at the time. Enron was an extremely profitable energy company based in Houston, Texas. Energy in the western United States is a business in which speculators buy a highly theoretical product like electricity at a specified time and for a specified amount and then resell it where there is need. The electricity is produced in a power plant and registered and put into the grid and held for a specified period of time. From there it is taken out for use hundreds of miles away, its price being determined by local conditions translated into demand. Speculators buy energy for themselves and bide their time until they get the highest price, for example during a heat wave in Los Angeles, when demand for energy is high and competing with similar demands in San Diego and San Francisco.

Because of the odd character of the business in which the product sold was neither fish nor fowl, neither a thing nor a service, in 1992 Enron was able to persuade the SEC to allow it to adopt an unorthodox accounting system called Mark-to-Market (MTM). To mount this operation, Enron formed a new company called the Enron Finance Corporation, appointed a man named Jeffrey Skilling its chief executive officer, and then operated separately from the mother company, even though it was only located on a different floor of the same building.

To say that Skilling then cooked the books is to put it mildly. He did so with the compliance of Arthur Andersen, one of the world's most reputable accountants. Andersen cooperated with Enron's maneuvers, which were chiefly concerned with speculative ventures which lost money but whose losses could be hidden in special purpose vehicles (SPVs), or off-book accounts that investors in Enron would not

15. From Brooksley Born to Sarbanes-Oxley

be allowed to see. In theory, Enron steadily lost money while its stock steadily rose.

Such operations were what the Securities and Exchange Commission (SEC) was created in 1934 to enable investors to avoid. The SEC has relatively straightforward reporting rules that over time companies have learned to circumvent by clever maneuvers. Mostly they fail because traditional cost accounting methods have also been honed to perfection in pursuit of the value of transparency. MTM provided a whole new world of opportunities, however.

Problems are more slippery when the corporation's product is energy, and they become even more complex with MTM accounting. Enron gamed the system and deceived the SEC by its use of the latter as well as SPVs to hide loses. Typically, Enron would sell a losing venture to one of its four raptor SPVs in return for money, thereby enabling itself continue looking good to investors, who would buy more stock and push its value higher on the market.

The SEC as well was deceived, but then in 2001 the company reported its first quarterly loss ever and also closed down its one of its four Raptor SPVs. This move caught the attention of the SEC, which began investigating Enron. One thing led to another as the SEC pulled away more veils and dug deeper into Enron's past. The more the SEC dug, the more the company's stock suffered on the market, and the more it plunged with the exposure of past losses. Real transparency meant the end for Enron.

Eventually, all of the top executives at Enron were arrested, accused of intentional wrongdoing, convicted, and imprisoned. One died of a heart-attack en route to conviction, another copped a plea and testified for the state, and a third, the company CEO Jeffrey Skilling, was convicted and sent to federal penitentiary for what amounted to a life sentence. In the midst of all this, the company's stock completely collapsed.

The moral of this story was similar to the one that Brooksley Born had been preaching in her many addresses to industry groups and Congress, namely, the need for an updated and modernized governmental operation to keep up with wrongdoing in the market. Congress had refused to accommodate Born and driven her out of Washington into premature retirement, but in the case of Enron the criminality of the operation was not so easy to avoid. Enron's special purpose vehicles were more than a little similar to mortgage backed securities in which SPVs like Countrywide could disguise losses—in its case subprime

Part Two—The Deregulated Society

borrowers—in packages that appeared to be sound but were not. The market, it would turn out seven years later, was filled with synthetic products that disguised the fact that their content was at best shaky and at worst corrupt from the outset.

If Enron has a positive side, it lay in the fact that Congress could not avoid the consequences of Enron's failure. In 2002 it passed legislation known by its sponsors names as Sarbanes-Oxley and even more compactly as SOX.[6] Most pieces of legislation are a reflection of the real-life situation they are trying to address and correct. Sarbanes-Oxley was no exception. In its section 302, Sarbanes-Oxley mandated that corporate executives certify in writing that a company's disclosure requirements met all SEC requirements. In other words, plausible deniability was henceforth made less plausible and in theory not plausible at all. In its section 404, Sarbanes-Oxley also provided that company management provide internal mechanisms to make certain that the disavowals executives signed off on actually worked on a day-to-day basis. Finally, in its section 802, Sarbanes-Oxley specified the kind of record-keeping practices a company had to follow, which mainly was a matter of what kind of records a company was obliged to keep and for how long.

Everything in the three sections named—section 302, 404, and 802—were reflections of what had been done at Enron and was conceivably being done at other companies. Crime is a matter of legal definition, and so if a crime is not defined as such in law, it is not a crime. When God put His Ten Commandments into writing, He was in effect identifying wrongdoing and willing the enforcement of measures to combat it. Sarbanes-Oxley was doing likewise.

◈◈◈

The question that confronts us here as elsewhere is whether consumer society could or would survive the radical shift away from New Deal financial arrangements that privileged local financial institutions and toward commercial banks that farmed out the mortgage business to those special purpose vehicles called mortgage brokers. Nowhere is the issue presented more sharply than in the career of Brooksley Born and the fate of the 2000 Commodities Futures Modernization Act. To all appearances, the law was the culmination of all that was desired by libertarians. They apparently placed their faith in the free (where *free* means free of regulation) market and registered that desire in a law that would prevent regulation now and in the future.

15. From Brooksley Born to Sarbanes-Oxley

In fact, however, they bet against themselves and so were prepared to pivot to an opposed position when caught out. This made clear in the documentary film *Inside Job*, when former president Bill Clinton claims he tried to persuade Alan Greenspan to moderate his position but failed. As filmmaker Charles Ferguson indicates, Clinton was lying to cover up his fundamentally important complicity in withholding the intervention needed to bolster Born's isolated position. With no backing whatsoever, her defeat was a foregone conclusion. Born rightly resigned from an administration that would not support its own appointee.

Passed in 2002, Sarbanes-Oxley might to said to have begun the process of reversing the wrongdoing promoted by the 2000 Commodities Futures Modernization Act, but if we are to judge by the facts of the 2008 financial crisis, it did not do nearly enough to confront the issue. Throughout, we do well to bear in mind that the business we are talking about is that of consumer society. Businesses are vehicles for the production and transmission of goods and services, and if management is allowed to deceive shareholders, then eventually and presumably, those shareholders with withhold their backing and take their power to finance elsewhere. We next proceed to see how Congress responded to the 2008 financial crisis.

16

Dodd-Frank and Legislative Approval of Consumer Society

Congressman turned Senator Carter Glass fully understood the politics of banking in his time. While embodying as much as any other man the South's suspicion of Wall Street, he also understood as well as James Madison of the seventh State of the Union address the necessity for some form of central banking. Carter Glass did the impossible by putting the two traditions together in one bill. It became the 1913 Owens-Glass Act, known to posterity as the Federal Reserve Act.[1]

Owens-Glass did two things that no one believed could be done in the same place at the same time. It shattered centralization in banking by making the Federal Reserve comprise 12 regional banks, with nearly as many in the South as in the North. But then it did something else that few persons paid adequate attention to. The Fed's requirement that regional banks hold reserves proportional to the holdings of its member banks meant that one of all twelve member banks, the one located a block away from Wall Street, held more reserves than the other eleven regional banks combined. In that way, Carter Glass preserved essence of central banking, but in the form of a regional bank.

In 2010, when Congressman Frank teamed up with Senator Dodd to author the Wall Street Reform and Consumer Protection Act, he confronted a task similar to that of Carter Glass a century earlier, namely, how to square the circle that he was confronted with.[2] His mandate was to pass legislation that would do what its title promised—reform Wall Street and protect the consumer. In a certain trivial sense, Congressman Frank could do a bit of both and make himself

16. Dodd-Frank and Legislative Approval of Consumer Society

look good. But such a modest achievement missed the crucial point: Frank's task was to reform Wall Street so effectively that consumer protection was not needed, or was needed only for the occasional mistakes of administrators.

I shall be arguing in this chapter that for a variety of reasons, Barney Frank was unable to perform the first task—reform Wall Street—and so he was compelled to invest heavily in the second task: protecting the consumer from the animal spirits on Wall Street.

The cornerstone of Dodd-Frank should have been an effort to eliminate the causes of the kind of collapse Wall Street experienced in 2007–2008. The authors of Dodd-Frank claimed to have done so by means of something called the *Financial Stability Oversight Council* (FSOC). But straight off, even with the name, we have an admission that the legislators responsible for Dodd-Frank did not intend any basic changes. They rather intended to accept things as they were but add to the existing system a dose of what Senator Dodd and Congressman Frank thought of as *stability*. The latter was actually in the interest of the big banks, so it seems reasonable to conclude, even at the outset, that the banks and AIG, the giant insurance company, might be in charge of the politics of this regulatory process.[3]

But if that was the case, then the big banks should have complained, because in respect to causes, the FSOC did not delivered even the little that Dodd-Frank promised.[4] The chair of the FSOC was the Secretary of the Treasury, a figure who is appointed by the president and who reports to him. That makes him or her a political figure.[5] The next nine permanent and voting members of the FSOC were heads of government agencies and so came to the FSOC representing their agencies and their interests. But even such a description misses the important point that one voting member, the Federal Reserve, was meant to be independent of politics. Are we to imagine that the FSOC was ever going to tell the chair of the Fed to raise or lower interest rates because the FSOC thought that was the appropriate thing to do? Is it not more likely that the chair of the Fed would consider the recommendation but consult his own board of governors before making any such move?

In other words, the FSOC was little more than an advisory council, or if the reader prefers, the elements of yet another interagency staff meeting mandated to consider nothing more weighty than the coordination of policy.

Next, take the seemingly smaller problem of the chair of the Commodity Futures Trading Commission (CFTC) being a permanent and voting member of the FSOC. We already saw that Treasury Secretary Robert E. Rubin could not dictate terms to Brooksley Born because she reported directly to the president and not to Treasury. Why should we now think that nearly ten years later the current head of the CFTC was going to bend to a committee headed by—you guessed it!—the Treasury secretary? The argument is likely to end up the same way that the 1998 quarrel between Rubin and Born ended up, namely, with Born doing what she deemed right regardless of Rubin's pressures.

I might be mistaken, but I don't see where a committee of ten more or less political appointees is capable of doing more than making narrow recommendations designed to affect small changes leading to stability.

The only proposal from Dodd-Frank that seemed to make sense was the Volcker Rule, proposed by former Fed Chairman Paul Volcker, to the effect that commercial banks should be prohibited from proprietary trading, or speculating in the financial markets, most especially with other people's money.[6] The rationale is that proprietary trading raises instability in the bank doing such trading, and so the activity, though profitable, is undesirable and should be prohibited.

But opinion on proprietary trading varies. President Obama favored the Volcker Rule, as did five different former secretaries of the treasury.[7] Commercial banks felt otherwise. They felt that proprietary trading gave them a competitive advantage over other banks, and they were able to use this to benefit their clients.

With such variation in opinion, the Volcker Rule ran into difficulty in becoming part of the final legislation. It was submitted in the Senate by Senators Jeff Merkley and Carl Levin as an amendment to the bill but was sidelined by a number of procedural moves proposed by Republicans. It only got into the bill at the conference level. But even there, Republican objections led to changes allowing commercial banks to invest in hedge funds and private equity funds. And then, after all was said and done, multiple bank presidents said that they didn't expect the rule to affect their profits much.[8]

Finally, to make matters worse for the FSOC, it is limited to a secretariat (staff) of approximately 25 persons and a secretarial budget of

16. Dodd-Frank and Legislative Approval of Consumer Society

approximately $10 million. In a city where worth is measured by the size of one's staff and budget, the FSOC secretariat was perilously close to being a joke. But even such a judgment fails to capture just how puny the authorized FSOC secretariat was, for it was not even adequate for the FSOC as originally proposed. To make up for its assumed shortcomings, the FSOC secretariat was authorized by borrow persons from involved agencies.

But such seconded[9] persons would continue to be paid by those agencies, which means that the borrowed staff members would not be loyal to the FSOC but rather to the home agencies that paid their salaries. In Washington, D.C., one licks the hand that feeds one, and in the case of the FSOC secretariat, that was often a hand that was located elsewhere in the city.

Apparently as a sop to the committee, Congress agreed to create a second entity called the Office of Financial Research (OFR). This weak agency is independent of other agencies but given that the OFR's mandate was circumscribed to conducting research on financial questions, it was likely to go to line agencies for its information and, doing so, was in immediate danger of being captured by the line agencies it was supposedly independent of. Furthermore, the OFR has no mandate to recommend action, and so the research floats free of purpose. It might be valuable, but without a statement of purpose there is no way to tell.[10]

It was originally hoped that the FSOC would be empowered to override agency action or inaction within its sphere of authority. Many in Congress opposed such a power, which would have created a super-agency with veto authority over lesser regulators. Instead, the FSOC was given the more limited authority to make recommendations for action and receive an explanation should the agency not accept those recommendations. This, needless to say, is not the power to do anything but is rather a mere advisory capacity.[11]

The conclusion is unusually drastic. The Financial Stability Oversight Council is one of those governmental agencies that is created because the times demand action but is constructed on the basis of internal contradictions so that meaningful action is precluded. Such an agency is one of the many sources of what critics call *red tape*, for it will no doubt seek to justify its existence by sending out questionnaires which may or may not be filled out, if they are returned at all. The red tape will then *gum up the works* insofar as the reports it generates will

Part Two—The Deregulated Society

be used in other agency staff meetings to support positions that have little to do with generating financial stability. The Financial Stability Oversight Council is unlikely to meet even the modest goals set for it in legislation.

◈◈◈

After Wall Street reform, the second formal element of the Dodd-Frank Act is consumer protection, to which end the law created the Consumer Financial Protection Bureau (CFPB). At the time of its creation, the person considered most likely to head the new bureau was Elizabeth Warren, but she presented three problems. The first was that she was the choice of President Barack Obama, and insofar as Republicans in Congress were inclined to block any and all Obama appointments, she was doomed from the start. The second problem was that Ms. Warren was a figure with no supporters who would defend her in more than nominal terms.

The third problem was and is more serious and transcends the person of Elizabeth Warren, although she represents it well.[12] Current law tends to approach mature consumer societies over two complementary but different approaches. The first is through *competition law*, which is concerned with maintaining the integrity of the market by keeping its players in effective competition with each other. The second is *consumer law*, which assumes without further question a market flawed by a lack of competition and puts all its resources into protecting the likely victim of this condition, namely, the consumer.[13] By temperament, Elizabeth Warren belonged to the latter school.

Therein lies a problem, however, for if the market is biased, then why not fix it rather than by-pass it to address the problems it generates? Why not address the causes rather than the effects? That question has already been answered in our consideration of the Financial Stability Oversight Council (FOSC), for that body was not given the structure to effectively make the market genuinely competitive. Therefore it was necessary to create the Consumer Financial Protection Bureau (CFPB). It amounted to including an admission of defeat built into the text of Dodd-Frank.

The latter thought provides us with an issue that is ongoing. To avoid litigation, businesses operating with written contracts tend to insert a clause in which a client agrees to resolve any disputes by arbitration. Without even discussing the drawbacks of arbitration, it needs to

16. Dodd-Frank and Legislative Approval of Consumer Society

be noted that such agreements are questionable because they are asking clients to forego their right to sue and use the public courts. The term *questionable* means that such a contract is potentially unconstitutional in that it is asking persons to waive rights.

An additional legal question had to do with class action suits, for litigation fees can only be met if litigation against a company are on behalf of all persons who suffer identical or sufficiently similar harms. If the action is on behalf of one person buying a faulty electric toothbrush, not enough money is involved and legal firms will not take up the challenge. Businesses generally object to class action suits, but it is hard to imagine how individual actions would work otherwise. For example, in respect to faulty airbags in automobiles, litigation must necessarily be class action.

President Obama held off appointing anyone until it became clear that Elizabeth Warren would not be approved. The president then shifted to a male, perhaps under the assumption that the Republicans were sexist, but in any case a man who was better connected than Warren. Nonetheless, the Republicans made it clear that they did not discriminate on gender grounds and so were as opposed to Richard Cordray as they had been to Elizabeth Warren. Obama therefore made a recess appointment of Cordray, a move that worked, but it didn't portend a happy experience for Cordray as head of the CFPB.

The issue intensified when Cordray suddenly resigned in November 2017.[14] President Trump attempted to appoint Mick Mulvaney his replacement, a move to which Cordray responded by appointing his deputy to be his permanent replacement, no doubt an unorthodox move and probably an illegal one as well.[15] Nonetheless, it indicated how fraught the situation was with Dodd-Frank.

The issue ends up in the air, but it is valuable for showing something of the logic of Republican opposition. Wealthy and established Republicans might not care one way of the other about the CFPB, but business people newly cutting into the market and intent upon making money from poor people without the interference of government regulators would be very interested in getting rid of a regulatory agency committed to enforcing the law. Hence, the very existence of the CFPB is chronically at stake. It is here that the expansion of the "free" market takes place.

❖❖❖

Part Two—The Deregulated Society

A third creation of Dodd-Frank was the Office of Credit Ratings (OCR), tasked with regulating private agencies like Standard and Poor's or Moody's that rate banks as well as their financial products or services. In the 2008 financial crisis, the rating agencies were said to have been a significant cause of the crisis because they failed to rate derivatives, especially the bundled mortgages that were called collateralized debt obligations (CDOs) or Mortgage Backed Securities (MBSs). They missed the extent to which the elementary particles of such packages were sub-prime mortgages.

I have argued the point before but a bit of repetition will do no harm. Imagine a CDO in which 10 percent of the mortgages bundled in it were sub-prime while the other 90 percent were prime. Arguably, any number of sub-prime failures would be buoyed up by the 90 percent of mortgages that were prime. But then imagine a CDO in which 90 percent of the mortgages were sub-prime. If half of those mortgages defaulted, that would most likely be enough to bring down the CDO. If these CDOs had been accurately assessed by the rating agencies, then the CDOs with 90 percent sub-prime mortgage content probably would not have sold.

The latter eventuality might have started a reverse effect in the market, initiated by banks watching what they were buying from mortgage brokers and refusing mortgages they could not package and sell. That in turn would have forced mortgage brokers like *Countrywide* to raise their standards and turn down applicants who could not meet the grade.

Commercial and investment banks had a certain kind of indeterminate knowledge of what brokers like *Countrywide* were sending them, enough to make them stop asking too many questions and instead buy insurance policies to cover themselves but not their products. The latter, called *swaps* were for the most part bought from the American International Group's (AIG) London office, run by a figure named Joe Cassano.[16] Being offshore, AIG was close to being unregulated and so did not keep anywhere near enough ready reserves to meet contingencies.

The problem with swaps was that (in theory) they covered the banks but not the purchasers of the CDOs. Assuming that AIG had enough reserves to cover some imagined disaster, they nonetheless still had no responsibility to end-users. My point in bringing this up is that this deficiency is that it could have been known in advance and probably was. The swaps were the rough equivalent of General Motors buying

16. Dodd-Frank and Legislative Approval of Consumer Society

insurance to cover themselves but not GM vehicles. The entire concept of swaps on CDOs or MBSs was similarly problematic.

Arguably, most of these dire consequences could have been avoided if existing credit rating agencies were not distorting the market, which they were. In the words of Moody's vice president Thomas McGuire, by "using securities ratings as a tool of regulation, [the government] fundamentally change[s] the nature of the product agencies sell. Issuers ... pay rating fees to purchase, not credibility with the investor community, but a license from a government."[17]

McGuire's last sentence was poorly written. It should read: "*Issuers of stocks should be paying rating fees to purchase transparency and credibility. Instead they are buying a license from a government.*" Nonetheless, his was a devastating critique, for if correct it meant that we'd all be better off if existing credit rating agencies were unregulated. But would an unregulated Standard and Poor's and Moody's have been an improvement? McGuire didn't think so. Hence, an officious sounding Office of Credit Ratings (OCR) was an unnecessary creation.

I closed the previous chapter with a complex but speculative opinion, namely, that the American people accepted the commercialization of consumer society but not in the unregulated form it appeared in during the financial crisis of 2008. Fairly clearly, it seemed to me, the popular opinion did not want a situation in which five or six commercial or investment banks were too big to fail, for that meant that they were running the government rather than the other way round. Again, it seemed fairly clear to me that the American people wanted the restoration of a situation in which a representative federal government had the final say over the kind of economy that characterized the United States.

I cannot help but harken back to Franklin D. Roosevelt's first inaugural address, in which the incoming president likened American society to a temple that had been invaded by money lenders who would henceforth be evicted from the premises. That work would be done by Senator Glass and Congressman Steagall, and so it came as no surprise that in 2008 numerous commentators saw fit to call for a restoration of Glass-Steagall or something like it. What they got instead was Dodd-Frank, and if this chapter has demonstrated anything, it is that Dodd-Frank was worse than nothing at all because it promised reform

Part Two—The Deregulated Society

in place of the kind of banishment from the temple that Glass-Steagall delivered. If proof was needed, it came in the form of the Consumer Protection Bureau, which from the outset assumed that the money lenders would stay in the temple and be up to their old tricks.

The conclusion to this chapter, then, amounts to a doubling down of what has been argued piecemeal in previous chapters. From the first deregulation of savings and loan institutions in 1980, the highly regulated consumer society that was heralded by *Time* magazine on July 3, 1950, has been replaced by the unregulated consumer society of the early 21st century. It is the same society, except under two different guises.

Conclusions:
The Consumer Paradise

The challenge of writing a conclusion to a book of this complexity is that of making it simple so as to contrast it with the book itself. To get anywhere near this goal, I would revert to the Introduction, where I claimed that the American people apparently have what they most want, which is ownership of a "box," the family home, where they can store the things they have delivered by Amazon. It helped to regulate the figurative "box," as was done from 1934 to 1980/1982, but it seems to work well enough in its deregulated state, which has been the case since 1980/1982.

Unless you believe that a law like Dodd-Frank is what controls the financial arrangements behind contemporary consumerism, you're likely to go along with popular naiveté and conclude that Wall Street is suddenly able to self-regulate. Carter Glass wouldn't have believed that, but it's been thirteen years since the big melt-down of 2008, and we're still at it, so something must be working.

I say this with some hesitation because I'm not particularly enamored of consumer society. My opinion doesn't matter, but to the extent that it's based on a vision of an alternative society, the counter argument is worth articulating. I made my version of it in the text of this book by invoking the image of a workers' party, not once but many times, and somewhat more vaguely an entire workers' society. But without conquering the state, neither of those visions is going to materialize, and there seems little chance of conquering the state if the candidates to lead the charge are the Republican or Democratic parties. They both underwrite capitalism, and the consumer society happens to be what they get. It's not particularly Marxist, but it is capitalist, and that's what counts.

Over the 87-year history of consumer society as I have defined it,

Conclusions: The Consumer Paradise

we have changed less than we think. Manufacturing still needs to be done and is done, only now in Guangdong province rather than in Michigan, and so if Marx was right about the center of the world being where the producers are, then it's shifted from Detroit to Guangzhou. Perhaps needless to say, a key power relation has changed in the most radical way, and we should at least understand what that means. Most likely China will not do anything dramatic to kill the goose that lays the golden eggs, but it will make small financial changes that will remind us where we stand in the pecking order, and those changes are unlikely to be for the better. Like Pinocchio, only collectively, we may be turning into a nation of donkeys, happy for getting our ice cream cones.

We have lost something, and if we have anybody to blame, then like Pogo we can say that we have met the enemy and he is us. We certainly shouldn't blame the Chinese. The consumer society is our doing, not theirs, and perhaps like the discovery of Carl Menger 150 years ago, it's only a matter of putting into place the final piece of a puzzle with an internal logic, marginal analysis, that was and still is irresistible. In that sense, the United States should serve as a warning to China: capitalism unfolds like a tropical flower, with production and muscular torsos coming first and consumerism, flab, and obesity only later. The United States is well on its way to completing that logic.

All of the above may be sour grapes on my part. If I get over my affliction and judge the consumer society I have described in this book, I could do worse than use the standards set forth by James Truslow Adams ninety years ago in *The Epic of America*. Adams was skeptical, as was Galbraith more than 22 years later, of what he perceived to be a gathering materialism. That much should have been obvious to the creators, and first of all to Winfield Riefler when he created the legislation that became the 1934 Housing Act. Home ownership was inappropriate to an ambient laboring class, but nonetheless it was what the federal government offered to the laborers of the embryonic CIO. Most everything was determined by that initial move, despite the fact that it would take two decades more to realize.

The racist exclusion of African Americans from the housing market was from its beginnings in Jim Crow society to its 1970s conclusions was a sideshow. Whether it was compounded with time or eliminated, racism did not affect the course of American consumerism. Once its direction was determined in 1934, there was no turning it away from its predetermined goal of greater and greater consumerism.

Conclusions: The Consumer Paradise

By a similar logic, so too the tectonic shift that occurred in 1980 changed nothing essential. Americans continued to buy homes and treat them as boxes in which they could store stuff until they burst or until additional storage space was rented outside the suburb where the houses were located. What happened after 1980 was the continuing deregulation of the consumer society, continuing right up to the present moment. To the extent that Dodd-Frank has any lasting meaning, it lies in the fact that Wall Street was reformed of criminal ways and consumers were henceforth protected from its worst excesses. There was not much more.

When all else is stripped away, this book boils down to the 1934 Housing Act and the model it provided for American consumer society. Get federally guaranteed ownership of a box in the suburbs of the nation's cities, fill it with purchases from the local warehouse, and then work two jobs to pay down the credit cards. The public character of such consumerism could even be stripped away, as it was in the last two decades of the last century, but essential American consumerism would still remain. It started as a bicycle with training wheels, the training wheels were taken off, until it is today the full-blown version of American society.

If the reader desires to see the future, he or she should visit Venice in Italy, for it is as perfected a version of the future as may be imagined. Everything in Venice is commercial, but few persons live there, and few of those who do are Italians. If that seems incredible, then look for the children. They are missing and are presumably somewhere on the nearby mainland. Look at the upper stories of Venice's buildings and ask if anyone lives there. Occasionally someone does, but more likely than not he or she is English or German and not Italian. And in a remarkable foretaste of global warming's effects, Venice's streets are waterways, not paved roads. Such will be the future fate of London and New York, but in Venice the reader can experience the future now and not have to wait for it to catch up with him or her.

Was all of this preordained? Was all of this written between the lines of the American Declaration of Independence? Is consumerism the final step in the pursuit of happiness? Was consumerism or at least the 18th century version of it what Hamilton meant Congress to hear with his message on credit? These are promising questions, but not for this book.

Chapter Notes

Chapter 1

1. See English, 2006. Her book was especially valuable in depicting not only the South but also the Northern textile city of Chicopee, Massachusetts, where the author of this book grew up.
2. Egerton, 1974.
3. Rove, 2015.
4. Berle and Means, 1932.
5. Arsene Pujo held hearings in 1913–14 on the "money trust" that caught the attention of the press and made it easier for Congress to pass financial reforms at the federal level.
6. I will call this the Berle argument for efficiency's sake. The shortening also has substantive value, however, since Means was mainly Berle's statistician. The argument was Berle's.
7. Pub. L. 80–201, 61 Stat. 136, became law on June 23, 1947 by votes overcoming the president's veto.

Chapter 2

1. Pub. L. 63–43, 38 Stat. 2 51, https://archive.org/stream/federalreserveac00idenrich/federalreserveac00idenrich_djvu.txt.
2. https://www.scribd.com/doc/73235213/Pecora-Commission-Report-Stock-Exchange-Practices-Report-1934.
3. Brandeis, 1914.
4. https://www.presidency.ucsb.edu/documents/campaign-address-progressive-government-the-commonwealth-club-san-francisco-california.
5. Freidel, 1954, pp. xx–xx. Apparently Freidel is the only biographer of Roosevelt to recognize the full significance of the Sept. 23, 1932 Commonwealth Club Address. Schlesinger, 1958, pp. 179–181 devotes three pages to the basic ideas but only two sentences to the Address.
6. Liaquat, 2009.
7. McCraw, 2012, ch. 10.
8. Hammond, 1957, chs. 13, 14.
9. Bray, 1957, ch. 17.
10. The Interstate Commerce Commission (ICC) was created in 1887.
11. The Food and Drug Administration (FDA) was created in 1906.
12. Keynes, 1922.

Chapter 3

1. Pub. L. 73–43, 48 Stat. 128, enacted June 13, 1933.
2. Harper Lee, *To Kill a Mockingbird* (New York: J.B. Lippencott, 1960).
3. The HOLA on Tuesday June 13 and Glass-Steagall on Friday, June 16.
4. NOLC Annual Report, 1933.
5. New Jersey at the time claimed to be the *Garden State*, but in fact name only meant that Jersey farmers produced items like carrots, lettuce and cucumbers that could readily be marketed in nearby New York City and Philadelphia.
6. HOLC Annual Report, 1933, p. 49.

Chapter 4

1. See a biographical entree on Riefler from the Richmond Federal Reserve

Notes—Chapter 4

Bank. https://www.richmondfed.org/publications/research/special_reports/treasury_fed_accord/bios/riefler/.

2. The letter is difficult to read at this point. Keynes may have met with Sen. Robert Bulkley of Ohio. My guess is that he met with Sen. Alben W. Barkley of Kentucky.

3. Letter: J.M. Keynes to W.R. Riefler, May 20, 1934, https://fraser.stlouisfed.org/files/docs/historical/nara/nara_riefler_1_05.pdf.

4. The gist of the issue is that ownership of *real* property is perilous for working class identification and so the leaders of that class should not allow it to happen. The essence of any durable definition of the middle class is ownership of real property (real estate) that stakes one to the value system of the middle class and that can be passed to one's offspring, creating a kind of immortality for the middle class.

5. Riefler also doubted the efficacy of the Hoover administration's Federal Home Loan Bank Act. "In an attempt to handle the problem on a broader basis the last Congress provided for the organization and expansion of the Home Loan Bank and Federal land bank systems. A relatively large amount of government funds has been made available to these institutions, but it is inadequate to take care of the billions of frozen mortgages that are in the picture. See Winfield W. Riefler, "Mortgage Situation" (Oct. 2, 1934), https://fraser.stlouisfed.org/files/docs/historical/nara/nara_riefler_1_05.pdf.

6. Winfield W. Riefler, *Money Rates and Money Markets in the United States* (New York: Harper & Brothers, 1930).

7. Winfield W. Riefler, "Mortgage Situation" (Oct. 2, 1934), https://fraser.stlouisfed.org/files/docs/historical/nara/nara_riefler_1_05.pdf.

8. Friedman and Jacobson, 1965.

9. Winfield W. Riefler, "Mortgage Situation" (Sept. 28, 1933), https://fraser.stlouisfed.org/files/docs/historical/nara/nara_riefler_1_05.pdf.

10. Berle and Means, 1932.

11. Brandeis, 1914.

12. One economist who did was Edwin R. A. Seligman of Columbia University (and of the storied Seligman family of Wall Street). In the early 1920s, Seligman was commissioned by General Motors to think through the social problem in installment buying. He did so and in 1927 published *The Economics of Installment Selling: A Study in Consumers' Credit, with Special Reference to the Automobile* (New York: Harper & Brothers, 1927). In his book, Seligman argued that there was no essential difference between production and consumption and that the established discourse was mainly a matter of Victorian moralizing. In order to clear the air, Seligman changed the established term "consumptive" (which suggested disease) to consumerism. He then argued the irreducible indeterminacy of claims about production and consumption. A captain of industry who authorizes the purchase of a new automobile to transport the company CEO is acting as a consumer as well as a producer, maybe even more so. A worker who buys a hearty breakfast for himself is fueling the engines of production as well as satisfying his longing for French toast. See Calder, 1999, pp. 237–261.

13. https://founders.archives.gov/documents/Hamilton/01-06-02-0076-0002-0001.

14. http://www.leninology.co.uk/2011/02/gramsci-on-americanism-and-fordism.html/.

15. Hans, 2007. https://www.lesonline.org/cv/AmalgamatedHousing.pdf.

16. Executive Order 7027, May 1, 1935. https://archive.org/details/4925387.1935.001.umich.edu/page/142/mode/1up.

17. Reblando, 2017. Reblando's book has an especially revealing collection of photographs.

18. Federal Housing Administration, *Technical Bulletin No. 4, Principles of Planning Small Houses* (U. S. Govt. Printing Office, 1936). See https://babel.hathitrust.org/cgi/pt?id=mdp.39015037428375;view=1up;seq=5/.

19. Loizides, Giorgios P., *Deconstructing Fordism: Legacies of the Ford Sociological Department* (2004). Dissertations. 1122, http://scholarworks.wmich.edu/dissertations/1122, p. 141.

Notes—Chapter 5

20. Federal Housing Administration, *Technical Bulletin No. 4, Planning of Small Houses* (U.S. Govt. Printing Office, 1936). See https://babel.hathitrust.org/cgi/pt?id=mdp.39015037428375;view=1up;seq=5/.

21. Adams, 1931.

22. So influential was this one concept of Adams that a book was written on it. See Cullen, 2004.

23. Well, of course, that was because it couldn't happen here, as Sinclair Lewis explained with uncanny timing in his novel, *It Can't Happen Here*. See Lewis, 1935.

24. Or alternately, Roosevelt was certain that his party base was the South and that the North was a thoroughly untrustworthy area, even Michigan and a city like Detroit.

25. The AFL was of course an umbrella organization, a federation of smaller craft unions and so itself not a union in the proper sense of the term. It is, however, easier to treat the term as a unity than to disaggregate it each time it is used. A similar reasoning applies to the CIO.

26. "Island Palms" was the original name of Levittown, NY.

27. The difference between conditions in 1934 and 1947 had to do with the down-payment. Many of the visitors to "Island Palms" were veterans for whom the amended 1945 GI Bill waived the down payment requirement.

Chapter 5

1. Pub. L. 73–67, 48 Stat. 195, effective June 16, 1933.

2. Title II of the act authorized the PWA.

3. In *Schechter v. United States*, 295 U.S. 495 (1935).

4. Public Housing Law §401. New York City public housing law is very confusing because it changes on average once every two years. This practice has enabled clever legislators to exploit the confusion for personal advantage. (The most notorious such exploitation was by Robert Moses in 1924.) For example, the following: "The New York City Housing Authority is hereby constituted and declared to be a body corporate and politic with all the powers, rights and duties set forth in article five of the former state housing law," which was a 1934 law "comprising §§ 60–78 of the former State Housing Law (L. 1926, ch. 823, as re-enacted by L. 1927, ch. 35), now the Public Housing Law (L. 1939, ch. 808)." Even these sentences are beyond the capabilities of a normal and healthy mind.

5. More or less, the Pale of Settlement comprised today's Poland, the western areas of Belarus, and western Ukraine.

6. Bauer, 1934.

7. The results are visible to the naked eye viewing Manhattan from Brooklyn's Williamsburg. The entire east River frontage from Stuyvesant Town to Delancey Street is occupied by public housing. In London, such housing would be in Becontree, in Paris in the "banlieue."

8. In a simplified form, this argument is bound to be controversial, for Europe's great cities had already experienced controversy over such questions, none more so than London with its post World War I "homes for heroes" project at Becontree east of (outside of) London. Becontree is the opposite of what Moses did in New York City, and it was nowhere near successful. The best example of what Bauer intended are the Queensborough Homes in Queens.

9. I am vastly simplifying a more complex story. Most of German-Austria was clerical and tending toward fascism. Vienna was the exception, and so the city's social democrats governed there but nowhere else. Because they were not full-blown Socialists, they did not overreach themselves as had the Bolsheviks of Budapest and Munich, who established "Soviet" republics. Vienna's social-democrats were also single-minded in their focus on housing.

10. Gruber, 1991.

11. Federal Housing Administration, *Technical Bulletin No. 4, Principles of Planning of Small Houses* (U. S. Govt. Printing Office, 1936). See https://babel.hathitrust.org/cgi/pt?id=mdp.390150374 28375;view=1up;seq=5/.

Notes—Chapters 6, 7 and 8

Chapter 6

1. 1938 National Housing Act: https://www.loc.gov/law/help/statutes-at-large/75th-congress/session-3/c75s3ch13.pdf/.
2. Brabner-Smith, 1938.
3. Which does not mean they are untrue. It is, however, implausible that legislation as comprehensive as the 1934 Housing Act would have omitted something as vital as providing for its future funding, if only as a promissory note.
4. The "deal" was initialed Sept. 2, 1940.

Chapter 7

1. Servicemen's Readjustment Act of 1944, Pub. L. 78–46, 38 Stat. 284M, effective June 22, 1944.
2. *Shelley v. Kraemer*, 334 U.S. 1 (1948).
3. Baxandall and Ewen, 2001 is the best general book on Levittown.
4. 43 Stat. 121, ch 157 (May 19, 1924).
5. Sect. 502, a–h.
6. Waller, 1944, p. 241. Waller's prose is purple but his insights into the minds of veterans are valuable.
7. Based on a calculation of $1.25 a day for overseas service and $1.00 for domestic service.
8. Lisio, 1974.
9. The Adjusted Compensation Payment Act (January 27, 1936, ch. 32, 49 Stat. 1099).
10. If an individual investor, and not a recognized lending agency makes the loan, the loan must obtain prior approval by the Veterans Administration in order for it to be guaranteed.
11. Pub. L. 79–601. It authorized a standing committee of 27 members and specified its jurisdictions, many of which ere kept by the Committee on Armed Services.
12. Katznelson, 2005.
13. Such an arrangement was in keeping with the practice of southern delegations in Congress of treating federal programs as limited by the reserve clause of the Constitution. The first and still best example was housing, which after 1937 was managed by local agencies such as the New York City Housing Authority (NYCHA) or the Chicago Housing Authority (CHA).
14. Although it was founded 27 years after the GI Bill was legislated, Liberty University of Lynchberg Virginia is a good example of this. Of its current enrollment of more than 15,000 students on campus, more than half are veterans, and more than half the courses offered at Liberty University are online and not in a classroom.

Chapter 8

1. https://iowaculture.gov/history/education/educator-resources/primary-source-sets/reconstruction-and-its-impact/booker-t.
2. 163 U.S. 537.
3. Harlan, 1986, pp. 71–120.
4. Du Bois, 1903.
5. Thomas Dixon, Jr., was the author of the original book, *The Clansman*, and was a friend of Woodrow Wilson while the two were students at the Johns Hopkins University.
6. W.R. Cash also viewed the protection of white women as the well-spring of southern society between the world wars.
7. *Buchanan v. Warley*, 245 U.S. 60 (1917).
8. I say evidently a follower of Du Bois because he was the most significant founder of the NAACP in 1909. His significance follows from his stated desire to challenge Jim Crow in the courts, which was the manifest purpose of the NAACP.
9. The literature on the internal migration of African Americans is not large but is excellent. See Lemann, 1992 and Wilkerson, 2010.
10. Myrdal, 1944.
11. See Liebow, 1967.
12. The 1941 wall begins across the street from the northern boundary of Van Antwerp Park, on Pembroke Avenue between Birwood and Mendota street. It extends north until just south of Eight Mile Road. See Sugrue, 1996.
13. Caro, 1974 is the Pulitzer winning biography of Moses. Everything I have

to say about Moses originates in Caro's book.

14. To date there is not a significant literature on this aspect of American politics. I have cobbled together what I know mainly from studies of manufacturing in the Boston area.

15. Moses graduated from Yale in 1909, Taft in 1910.

16. Bauer, 1934.

17. Riis, 1904. Riis's book is mainly photographs but is all the more powerful for that.

Chapter 9

1. Baxendall, 2000.
2. Such a technique had been used before, initially perhaps in Lowell, Massachusetts, 120 years earlier. In 1850 it was used in Holyoke, Massachusetts, to build that city.
3. Gruen, 1965.
4. Gladwell, 2004.
5. Sorkin, 1992.

Chapter 10

1. Werner Sombart.
2. This was Werner Sombart's question.
3. Dies are the forms that are attached to presses for the making of the parts of the automobile chassis: the doors, roof, hood, trunk, etc. These parts are assembled out of rolled-steel arriving from Pittsburgh, Cleveland or Youngstown in Ohio. The workers who make the dies are the most highly skilled and paid in the automotive industry. The quarters where they work are clean and well-equipped with the full variety of cutting and measuring tools needed to make the dyes. The tool and die makers, as they are called, are the aristocracy of the industrial working class.
4. The laborers at Flint most likely understood the significance of the building where GM's dyes were made and stored, but if they had any doubt at all, it would have been dispelled by Reuther, who fully comprehended the significance

of any building that held a company's dyes.

5. Lichtenstein, 1995, ch 14, pp. 299–326, where Lichtenstein describes Reuther as a leader unable to act because of a systematically inadequate social consciousness on the part of UAW members.

Chapter 11

1. Myrdal, 1944.
2. *Sweatt v. Painter*, 339 U.S. 629 (1950).
3. *McLaurin v. Oklahoma State Regents*, 339 U.S. 637 (1950).
4. *Brown v. Board of Education of Topeka*, 347 U.S. 483 (1954).
5. Woodward, C. Vann, *The Strange Career of Jim Crow* (New York: Oxford University Press, 1955).
6. Claudette Colvin was the first African American to so refuse, but for understandable social reasons, Montgomery's civil rights lawyers declined to pursue her case and waited for a socially more acceptable case, which Rosa Parks provided.
7. Ransby, 2003.
8. I am repeating here a criticism of Ella Baker, who very early was skeptical of the type of movement being set up by Dr. King. Her apparent fear was that the SCLC would over time become too conservative.
9. The Chicago Freedom Movement was a coalition of the Coordinating Council of Community Organizations (CCCO), the Southern Christian Leadership Conference (SCLC), and the American Friends Service Committee (AFSC).
10. 90–284, 82 Stat. 73, signed April 11, 1968.
11. Satter, 2009, pp. 98–99.
12. 90–284, 82 Stat. 73, signed April 11, 1968.
13. Another was the young Barack Obama, but he came later.
14. 15 U.S.C. § 1691, enacted 28 Oct 1974.
15. https://www.law.cornell.edu/cfr/text/12/1002.1.
16. Pub. L. No. 94–200; 89 Stat. 1124), effective12/31/75, 12 USC 2801.
17. Pub. L. 95–128, 91 Stat. 1147, Title

VIII of the Housing and Community Development Act of 1977, 12 USC para. 2901.
18. Stein, 2010.
19. Stein 2010 again, but this time nothing that Prof. Stein wrote missed the significance of changing lending standards at the nation's S&Ls.

Chapter 12

1. The best primer for this period is Dutton, 1971.
2. The 11% number is correct but misleading. In states like Illinois, New York or Michigan that counted more on the electoral map, the percentage of African Americans eligible to vote was much higher than 11%. The problem lay in mobilizing this vote.
3. To synopsize only Jackson's domestic platform, it would create *jobs* in order to rebuild the nation's infrastructure; combat *drugs* by prosecuting suppliers rather than users; create a *single-payer* system of medicine; strictly enforce *voting rights*; increase funding for *elementary education*; and support ratification of the E. R. A. for women.
4. The memo was addressed to Eugene Sydnor, Jr., and the United States Chamber of Commerce and dated August 23,1971. For the full text, see https://scholarlycommons.law.wlu.edu/powellmemo/1/.
5. For excellent background to the memo, see Schmitt, 2005. Among other things, Schmitt raises the question whether the *Powell Memo* ever had any of the significance later assigned to it by historians looking for some kind of literary genesis to a moment they could not otherwise explain.
6. From was executive director of the House Democratic Caucus from 1981 to 1985. During 1979 and 1980, From was deputy advisor on inflation to President Jimmy Carter, and from 1971 to 1979, he directed the U.S. Senate Subcommittee on Intergovernmental Relations.
7. From, 2013, especially ch. 6, pp. 67–84. The book is also one of the best on the internal workings of the Clinton administration. See chs. 15, 16, and 17.

Chapter 13

1. Simon, 1978, for background.
2. The leveraged buy-out began in January 1981, and the process of moving from public to private and then back again to a public company lasted for about 18 months.
3. Kosman, 2009. Kosman is tendentious but generally well-informed and accessible in respect to private equity at the turn of the century.
4. Boston's banks in the 1850s were stocked with money earned from mills in Lowell and Lawrence. Besides the Suffolk Bank using its money to finance a machine-tool company founded by Paul Moody, it facilitated the purchase of machinery from Moody's company by acting as a clearing house for payment from local banks elsewhere in southern New England. In this manner just about every town in Massachusetts, Connecticut, and Rhode Island with the name "Falls" in its title was industrialized.
5. In March 2020, Bain was ranked by *Investopedia* as the 6th largest private equity company in the world. See https://www.investopedia.com/articles/markets/011116/worlds-top-10-private-equity-firms-apo-bx.asp.
6. Black, 2005.
7. A similar advertisement for banks in Mesquite, Texas, ran on Aug, 13, 2020, or as this chapter was being written. See *Best Cash Cow* at https://www.bestcashcow.com/savings-accounts/rates-tx-mesquite.
8. Alan Pusey, "Fast Money and Fraud," *New York Times*, April 23, 1989.
9. Faulkner began his operation by buying otherwise useless land along the I-30 corridor and laying out seductive golf courses and plots for homes depicted in architects' drawings as luxurious. Then, as frosting on the cake, Faulkner learned to fly a helicopter so that he to show his property to prospective clients from the air. He was, needless to say, a great success.
10. Pub. L. 97–320, 96 Stat. 1469, signed October 15, 1982.
11. 97–320, 96 Stat. 1469, signed Oct. 15, 1982.

Notes—Chapters 14, 15 and 16

Chapter 14

1. Pub. L. 106–102, 113 Stat. 1338, enacted Nov. 12, 1999.
2. Gramm, 1982.
3. The bill's third author, Cong. Thomas J. Bliley, Jr., did not play a significant role in the bill's career.
4. https://www.youtube.com/watch?v=R3896I5pSxE/.
5. Approximately 20:00 minutes into the Moyers' interview.
6. Robert E. Rubin, with Jacob Weinberg, *In an Uncertain World: Tough Choices from Washington to Wall Street* (New York: Random House, 2004) for Rubin's side of the story.
7. That Rubin was the Washington counterpart to Sandy Weill and John Reed in New York was affirmed after the repeal of Glass-Steagall when he left the government and found employment at—it's easy to guess—Citigroup. Rubin would go on to spend the next ten years there, collecting more than $100 million in bonuses along the way. Even by current Wall Street standards, that was a great deal of money for a man who did not have a line position at Citigroup.
8. NINJA=No Income, no job (no) anything.
9. For background, I am obliged to Charles Ferguson's *Inside Job: The Financiers Who Pulled off the Heist of the Century* (Oxford: Oneworld Publications, 2012).
10. In 2006, New Century had more than 7,100 employees and 222 sales offices nationwide. The company originated home mortgage loans designed for subprime borrowers. In 1996, the company originated over $350 million in loans. In 1997, New Century went public and was listed on the New York Stock Exchange. In 2001, the company's subprime loan origination volume exceeded $6 billion. Volume continued to grow rapidly, and volume increased tenfold to over $50 billion in 2006.
11. Carr, James H., and Jenny Schuetz, "Financial Services in Distressed Communities: Framing the Issue, Finding Solutions" (Wash., D.C.: Fannie Mae Foundation, 2001). See also Antje Berndt Burton Hollifield Patrik Sandås, "The Role of Mortgage Brokers in the Subprime Crisis," NBER Working Paper Series, https://www.nber.org/papers/w16175.pdf.
12. William Heisel, "U.S. Banking Official Darrel Dochow Retiring After Furor Over IndyMac Failure," *Los Angeles Times*, Feb. 21, 2009. See https://www.latimes.com/archives/la-xpm-2009-feb-21-fi-dochow21-story.html/.
13. Black, 2005.
14. Section 38 of the Federal Deposit Insurance Act (FDI Act) (12 USC 1831).

Chapter 15

1. He chose Janet Reno instead.
2. Rubin, 2003, p. 287. Remarkably for a book that looks autobiographical, Rubin mentions Born only once and the CFTC not at all.
3. See http://www.cftc.gov/opa/speeches/opabbtes4.htm/.
4. https://www.cftc.gov/sites/default/files/opa/speeches/opaborn-45.htm/. On May 7, Born delivered remarks to the Finance and Society Conference. See https://wallstreetonparade.com/2015/05/brooksley-born-still-telling-the-uncomfortable-truths-about-wall-street/.
5. H. R. 4541, 106th Congress, Oct. 19, 2000. This is the House citation for the CFMA. The most advanced version of the Senate bill was S 2697. It was signed into law on Dec. 21, 2000, or in the lame duck period of the Clinton presidency.
6. Pub. L. 107–204, 107th Congress, HR 3763, 15 USC 7201.

Chapter 16

1. Pub. L. 63–43, 38 Stat. 251, signed Dec. 23, 1913.
2. Pub. L. 111–203, H.R. 4173.
3. AIG was named a "Systemically Important Financial Institution" by the FSOC but had this label rescinded by a vote of 6 to 3 in late Sept. 2017. See *Wall Street Journal*, Sept. 30–Oct. 1, 2017, p. 1. The label entailed added federal regulation. With its removal, regulatory

171

Notes—Chapter 16

oversight continued with the New York state Department of Financial Services.

4. A place to start is with Hilary J. Allen's "Putting the 'Financial Stability' in Financial Stability Oversight Council," *Ohio State Law Journal*, v. 75:5, http://moritzlaw.osu.edu/students/groups/oslj/files/2016/01/Vol.-76_5–1087–1152-Allen-Article.pdf/.

5. See David Skeel, *The New Financial Deal: Understanding the Dodd-Frank Act and Its (Unintended) Consequences* (New York: Wiley, 2011), ch. 3.

6. Section 619 of Dodd-Frank.

7. *Wall Street Journal*, Feb. 22, 2010.

8. https://www.thestreet.com/story/10860335/1/bofa-ceo-says-volcker-rule-wont-be-too-tough.html?cm_ven=GOOGLEFI/.

9. A commonly used British term indicating a practice in the British government, but one that is problematic in that such persons act as spies for the agency that is paying them.

10. See Simon Johnson, "The Disappointing Office of Financial Research," *New York Times* (Jan. 30, 2014), http://economix.blogs.nytimes.com/2014/01/30/the-disappointing-office-of-financial-research/?_r=1.

11. Daniel K. Tarullo, "Remarks at the University of Pennsylvania Law School Distinguished Jurist Lecture," Financial Stability Regulation (Oct. 10, 2012), transcript available at http://www.federalreserve.gov/news events/speech/tarullo20121010a.htm. Unfortunately, Tarullo's 'Remarks' lack pagination. See his comment on the third to last paragraph of the 'Remarks,' from which I take Tarullo's words verbatim.

12. See Elizabeth Warren's "The Vanishing Middle Class," in John Edwards, ed., *Ending Poverty in America: How to Restore the American Dream* (New York: The New Press, 2007). See also Warren's video, "The Coming Collapse of the Middle Class," https://www.youtube.com/watch?v=akVL7QY0S8A/.

13. See Katalin Judit Cseres, *Competition Law and Consumer Protection* (The Hague: Kluwer Law International, 2005).

14. https://www.nytimes.com/2017/11/15/business/cordray-consumer-protection.html?_r=0/.

15. https://www.nytimes.com/2017/11/24/us/politics/onsumer-financial-protection-bureau-cordray-leader-trump-mulvaney.html?_r=0/.

16. See Matt Taibbi, "The Big Takeover," *Rolling Stone*, March 23, 2009.

17. Thomas McGuire, "Ratings in Regulation: A Petition to the Gorillas," speech at the SEC's fifth annual International Institute for Securities Market Development, April 2, 1995.

Bibliography

Adams, James Truslow, *The Epic of America* (Boston: Little, Brown & Co., 1931).
Ahamed. Liaquat, *Lords of Finance, The Bankers Who Broke the World* (New York: Penguin Books, 2009).
Altschuler, Glenn C., and Stuart M. Blumin, *The GI Bill: A New Deal for Veterans* (New York: Oxford University Press, 2009).
Amis, Martin, *Money* (London: Jonathan Cape, 1984).
Applebome, Peter, *Dixie Rising: How the South Is Shaping American Values, Politics, and Culture* (New York: Harcourt Brace, 1996).
Austen, Ben, "The Towers Went Down, and with Them Went the Promise of Public Housing," *New York Times*, Feb. 7, 2018.
Baer, Kenneth S., *Reinventing Democrats: The Politics of Liberalism from Reagan to Clinton* (Lawrence: University Press of Kansas, 2000).
Ballon, Hilary, "Robert Moses and Urban Renewal," in Hilary Ballon and Kenneth T. Jackson, *Robert Moses and the Modern City: The Transformation of New York* (New York: Norton, 2007).
Ballon, Hilary, ed., *The Greatest Grid: The Master Plan of Manhattan 1811–2011* (New York: Museum of the City of New York and Columbia University Press, 2013).
Bank of England, *Money Creation in the Modern Economy* (London: 2014).
Barnard, John, *American Vanguard: The United Auto Workers During the Reuther Years, 1935–1970* (Detroit: Wayne State University Press, 2004).
Barnard, John, *Walter Reuther and the Rise of the Auto Workers* (Boston: Little Brown, 1983).
Bauer, Catherine, *Modern Housing* (Cambridge: Riverside Press, 1934).
Bauer, Catherine, "The Social Front of Modern Architecture in the 1930s," *Journal of the Society of Architectural Historians*, March 1965.
Baxandall, Rosalyn, and Elizabeth Ewen, *Picture Windows: How the Suburbs Happened*. (New York: Basic Books, 2000).
Beito, David, *Taxpayers in Revolt* (Chapel Hill: University of North Carolina Press, 1989), pp. 11–15 on NAREB as national lobbying group.
Ben-Joseph, Eran, and Terry S. Szold, *Regulating Place, Standards and the Shaping of Urban America* (New York: Rutledge, 2005).
Berle, Adolf, and Gardiner C. Means, *The Modern Corporation and Private Property* (New York: Harcourt, Brace & World, 1932).
Bernays, Edward, *Crystalizing Public Opinion* (New York: Boni and Liveright, 1923).
Bernays, Edward, *Propaganda* (New York: Horace Liveright, 1928).
Black, William K., *The Best Way to Rob a Bank Is to Own One* (Austin: University of Texas Press, 2005).
Bloom, Nicolas D., *Public Housing That Worked: New York in the Twentieth Century* (Philadelphia: University of Pennsylvania Press, 2008).

Bibliography

Boyle, Kevin, *The UAW and the Heyday of American Liberalism 1945–1968* (Ithaca: Cornell University Press, 1995).
Brabner-Smith, J. W., "The National Housing Act Amendments of 1938," *American Bar Association Journal*, vol. 24, no. 8, April 1938.
Brandeis, Louis, *Other People's Money and How Bankers Use It* (New York: Stokes, 1914).
Breen, T. H., *The Marketplace of Revolution: How Consumer Politics Shaped American Independence* (New York: Oxford, 2004).
Brewer, John, *The Sinews of Power: War, Money, and the English State, 1688–1783* (Cambridge, MA: Harvard University Press, 1988).
Burns, Leland S., and Leo Grebler, *The Housing of Nations: Analysis and Policy in a Comparative Framework* (New York: Wiley, 1977).
Cahill, Kevin, *Who Owns Britain* (London: Canongate Books, 2000).
Calder, Lendol, *Financing the American Dream: A Cultural History of Consumer Credit* (Princeton: Princeton University Press, 1999).
Cam, Gilbert A. "United States Government Activity in Low-Cost Housing, 1932–38," *Journal of Political Economy*, vol. 47, No. 3 (June 1939).
Caro, Robert, *The Power Broker: Robert Moses and the Fall of New York* (New York: Random House-Vintage, 1974).
Carter, Susan B., et al, *Historical Statistics of the United States* (New York: Cambridge University Press, 2006).
Cash, W.J., *The Mind of the South* (New York: Random House/Vintage, 1941).
Chancellor, Edward, "The Long Shadow of the Austrian School," *New York Review of Books*, May 14, 2020.
Chandler, Lester V., *Benjamin Strong: Central Banker* (Washington, D.C.: Brookings Institution, 1968).
Cockett, Richard, *Thinking the Unthinkable: Think-Tanks and the Economic Counter-Revolution, 1931–1983* (New York: Fontana Press, 1995).
Cohen, Lizabeth, *A Consumers' Republic: The Politics of Mass Consumption in Postwar America* (New York: Vintage Books, 2003).
Cohen, Lizabeth, *Making a New Deal: Industrial Workers in Chicago, 1919–1939* (New York: Cambridge University Press, 1990).
Cullen, Jim, *The American Dream: A Short History of an Idea That Shaped a Nation* (New York: Oxford University Press, 2004).
Dayen, David, *Chain of Title: How Three Ordinary Americans Uncovered Wall Street's Great Foreclosure Fraud* (New York: The New Press, 2017).
Desmond, Matthew, *Evicted: Poverty and Profit in the American City* (New York: Penguin/Random House, 2016).
Drehle, David Von, *Triangle: The Fire That Changed America* (New York: Atlantic Monthly Press, 2003).
Du Bois, W. E. B., *The Souls of Black Folk* (Chicago: A. C. McClurg & Co., 1903).
Dutton, Frederick G. *Changing Sources of Power: American Politics in the 1970s* (New York; McGraw-Hill, 1971).
Eccles, George S., *The Politics of Banking* (Salt Lake City: University of Utah Press, 1982).
Egerton, John, *The Americanization of Dixie: The Southernization of America.* (New York: Harper's Magazine Press, 1974).
Eisenstadt, Peter, *Rochdale Village: Robert Moses, 6,000 Families, and New York City's Great Experiment in Integrated Housing* (Ithaca, NY: Cornell University Press, 19xx).
Elias, Norbert, *The Civilizing Process* (Oxford: Blackwell, 1994).
English, Beth, *A Common Thread: Labor, Politics, and Capital Mobility in the Textile Industry* (Athens, GA: University of Georgia Press, 2006).
Evans, M. Stanton, *The Liberal Establishment* (New York: Devin-Adair Pub. Co., 1965).
Fabozzi, Frank J., and Franco Modigliani, *Mortgage and Mortgage-backed Securities Markets* (Cambridge, MA: Harvard Business School Press, 1992).
Federal Housing Administration, *Technical Bulletin No. 4, Planning of Small Houses*

Bibliography

(Washington, D.C.: US Govt. Printing Office, 1936). See https://babel.hathitrust.org/cgi/pt?id=mdp.39015037428375;view=1up;seq=5/.

Ferguson, Charles, *Inside Job: The Financiers Who Pulled off the Heist of the Century* (Oxford: Oneworld Publications, 2012).

Ferré-Sadurni, Luis, "The Rise and Fall of New York Public Housing," *New York Times*, July 9, 2018.

Fishback, Price, Jonathan Rose, and Kenneth Snowden. *Well Worth Saving: How the New Deal Safeguarded Home Ownership*, 1st ed. (University of Chicago Press, 2013).

Fitz-Gibbon, Desmond, *Marketable Values: Inventing the Property Market in Modern Britain* (University of Chicago Press, 2019).

Florida, Richard, *The New Urban Crisis: How Our Cities Are Increasing Inequality, Deepening Segregation, and Failing the Middle Class* (New York: Basic Books, 2017).

Florida, Richard, *The Rise of the Creative Class, and How its Transforming Work, Leisure, Community, and Everyday Life* (New York: Basic Books, 2002).

Frank, Thomas, *The People, No: A Brief History of Anti-Populism* (New York: Henry Holt, 2020).

Freidel, Frank, *Rendez Vous with Destiny* (Boston: Little Brown, 1990).

Friedman, Milton, and Anna Jacobsen Schwartz, *The Great Contraction, 1929–1933* (Princeton, NJ: Princeton University Press, 2008).

From, Al, *The New Democrats and the Return to Power* (New York: St. Martin's Press, 2013).

Gaddis, John Lewis, *George F. Kennan: An American Life* (New York: Penguin Press, 2011),

Galbraith, James K., *The Predator State* (New York: Basic Books, 2008).

Galbraith, John K., *The Affluent Society* (Boston: Houghton Mifflin, 1958).

Galbraith, John K., *American Capitalism: The Theory of Countervailing Power* (Boston: Houghton Mifflin, 1952).

Gabraith, John K. *The New Industrial State* (Boston: Houghton Mifflin, 1967).

Galloway, Scott, *The Four: The Hidden DNA of Amazon, Facebook, Apple, and Google* (New York: Penguin/Random House, 2017).

Gans, Herbert, *The Levittowners: Ways of Life and Politics in a New Suburban Community* (New York: Columbia University Press, 1967).

Giridharadas, Anand, *Winners Take All: The Elite Charade of Changing the World* (New York: Alfred A, Knopf, 2018).

Gladwell, Malcalm, "The Terrazzo Jungle," *The New Yorker*, March 15, 2004.

Glaeser, Edward, *Triumph of the City: How Our Best Invention Makes Us Richer, Smarter, Greener, Healthier, and Happier* (New York: Penguin Press, 2011).

Glickman, Lawrence B., *Buying Power: A History of Consumer Activism in America* (University of Chicago Press, 2009).

Glickman, Lawrence B., *Consumer Society in America: A Reader* (Ithaca: Cornell University Press, 1999).

Golembe, Carter H., "The Deposit Insurance Legislation of 1933: An Examination of Its Antecedents and Its Purposes," *Political Science Quarterly*, vol. 74, June 1960.

Graeber, David, *Debt: The First 5000 Years* (New York; Melville House, 2011).

Gramm, Phil, *The Role of Government in a Free Society* (Irvington, NY: Fisher Institute, 1982).

Grebler, Leo, David M. Blank, and Louis Winnick, *Capital Formation in Residential Real Estate: Trends and Prospects* (Princeton: Princeton University Press, 1956).

Gruber, Helmut, *Red Vienna: Experiment in Working Class Culture, 1919–1934* (New York: Oxford University Press, 1991).

Gruen, Victor, *The Heart of Our Cities: The Urban Crisis: Diagnosis and Cure* (London: Thames & Hudson, 1965).

Hacker, Jacob S., and Paul Pierson, *Winner–Take-All-Politics* (New York: Simon & Schuster, 2010).

Bibliography

Hammond, Bray, *Banks and Politics in America: From the Revolution to the Civil War* (Princeton: Princeton University Press, 1957).
Hanchett, Thomas, "US Tax Policy & the Shopping Center Boom of the 1950s and 1960s," *American Historical Review* (October 1996).
Hans, Alexandra Vozick, https://www.lesonline.org/cv/AmalgamatedHousing.pdf.
Hardwick, M. Jeffrey, *Mall Maker: Victor Gruen, Architect of an American Dream* (Philadelphia: University of Pennsylvania Press, 2003).
Harlan, Louis R., *Booker T. Washington: The Wizard of Tuskegee, 1901–1915* (New York: Oxford University Press, 1986).
Harriss, C. Lowell, "Background of the Home Owners' Loan Corporation Legislation," http://www.nber.org/chapters/c3206.pdf
Harriss, C. Lowell, *History and Policies of the Home Owners Loan Corporation* (New York: National Bureau of Economic research, 1951).
Hayden, Dolores, *Building Suburbia, Green Fields and Urban Growth, 1820–2000* (New York: Vintage Books, 2003).
Hendrickson, Jill M., "The Long and Bumpy Road to Glass-Steagall Reform, A Historical and Evolutionary Analysis of Banking Legislation," *American Journal of Economics and Sociology*, vol. 60, no. 4, Oct. 2001.
Herman, Arthur. *Freedom's Forge: How American Business Produced Victory in World War II* (New York: Random House, 2012).
Hersey, John, *The Algiers Motel Incident* (New York: Alfred A. Knopf, 1968).
Hirsch, Arnold R., *Making the Second Ghetto: Race and Housing in Chicago, 1940–1960* (University of Chicago Press, 1983).
Hoffman, Alexander von, "Study in Contradictions: The Origins and Legacy of the Housing Act of 1949," https://www.innovations.harvard.edu/sites/default/files/hpd_1102_hoffman.pdf
Hoffman, Nicholas von, *Radical: A Portrait of Saul Alinsky* (New York: Nation Books, 2010).
Hofstadter, Richard, "From Calhoun to the Dixiecrats," *Social Research* 16 (June 1949).
Hollis-Brusky, Amanda, *Ideas with Consequences: The Federalist Society and the Conservative Counterrevolution* (New York: Oxford University Press, 2015).
Horowitz, Daniel, *Consuming Pleasures: Intellectuals and Popular Culture in the Postwar World* (Philadelphia: University of Penn Press, 2012).
Horowitz, Daniel, *The Morality of Spending: Attitudes Toward Consumer Society in America, 1875–1940* (Lanham, MD: Ivan Dee, 1985).
Howe, Irving, *World of Our Fathers* (New York: Harcourt, Brace, Jovanovich, 1976)
Humes, Edward, *Over Here: How the GI Bill Transformed the American Dream* (New York: Harcourt, 2006).
Hyman, Louis, *Debtor Nation: The History of America in Red Ink* (Princeton: Princeton University Press, 2011).
Jackson, Kenneth T., *Crabgrass Frontier: The Suburbanization of the United States* (New York: Oxford, 1985).
Jacobs, James A., *Detached America: Building Houses in Postwar Suburbia* (Charlottesville: University of Virginia Press, 2015).
Jacobs, Jane, *The Death and Life of Great American Cities* (New York: Random House, 1961).
Joint Center for Housing Studies of Harvard University, *The State of the Nation's Housing, 2017* (Cambridge, MA: JCHS, 2017).
Jones, Daniel Stedman, *Masters of the Universe: Hayek, Friedman, and the Birth of Neo-liberal Politics* (Princeton, NJ, Princeton University Press, 2012).
Judis, John B., *The Paradox of American Democracy: Elites, Special Interests, and the Betrayal of Public Trust* (New York: Rutledge, 2006).
Kane, Edward J. *The S&L Insurance Mess: How Did It Happen?* (Washington, D.C.: The Urban Institute, 1989).

Bibliography

Katona, George, *Psychological Analysis of Economic Behavior* (New York: McGraw-Hill, 1951).
Katznelson, Ira, *When Affirmative Action Was White* (New York: Norton, 2005).
Key, V.O., *Southern Politics in State and Nation* (New York: Knopf, 1949).
Keynes, John Maynard, *The Consequences of the Peace* (London: Macmillan, 1919).
Keynes, John Maynard, *A Tract on Monetary Reform* (London: Macmillan, 1922) (Collected Works, vol. IV).
Koch, Charles G., *The Science of Success: How Market-Based Management Built the World's Most Successful Company* (New York: Wiley, 2007).
Kosman, Josh, *The Buyout of America: How Private Equity Is Destroying Jobs and Killing the American Economy* (New York: Penguin, 2009).
Kynaston, David, *Austerity Britain, 1945–1951* (New York: Walker Publishing, 2008).
Lafer, Gordon, *The One-Percent Solution* (Ithaca: Cornell University Press, 2017).
Lane, Barbara Miller, *Houses for a New World: Builders and Buyers in American Suburbs, 1945–1965* (Princeton, NJ: Princeton University Press, 2015).
Lears, Jackson, *Fables of Abundance: A Cultural History of Advertising in America* (New York; Basic Books, 1994).
Leavitt, Jacqueline. "The Interrelated History of Cooperatives and Public Housing from the Thirties to the Fifties," *The Hidden History of Housing Cooperatives*, edited by Allan Heskin and Jacqueline Leavitt (Davis: Center for Cooperatives, University of Calif., 1995).
Lemann, Nicholas, *The Promised Land: The Great Black Migration and How It Changed America* (New York: Alfred A. Knopf, 1991).
Lewis, Sinclair, *It Can't Happen Here* (New York: Doran & Co., 1935).
Liaquat, Ahamed, *Lords of Finance: The Bankers Who Broke the World* (New York: Penguin Books, 2009).
Lichtenstein, Nelson. *The Most Dangerous Man in Detroit: Walter Reuther and the Fate of American Labor* (New York: BasicBooks, 1995).
Lipsitz, George, *Rainbow at Midnight: Labor and Culture in the 1940s* (Urbana: University of Illinois Press, 1994).
Lisio, Donald J., *The President and Protest: Hoover, Conspiracy, and the Bonus Riot* (Columbia: University of Missouri Press, 1974).
Loewen, James, *Sundown Towns: A Hidden Dimension of American Racism* (New York: Touchstone Books, 2005).
Loizides, Giorgios P., *Deconstructing Fordism: Legacies of the Ford Sociological Department (2004). Dissertations. 1122.* http://scholarworks.wmich.edu/dissertations/1122
Loomis, Erik, *A History of American Labor in Ten Strikes* (New York: The New Press, 2018).
Martin, Isaac William, *Rich People's Movements: Grassroots Campaigns to Untax the 1%* (New York: Oxford University Press, 2013).
Massey, Douglas S., and Nancy A. Denton, *American Apartheid: Segregation and the Making of the Underclass* (Cambridge, MA: Harvard University Press, 1998).
Mayer, Jane, *Dark Money: The Hidden History of the Billionaires Behind the Rise of the Radical Right* (New York: Doubleday, 2016).
Mayer, Martin, *The Greatest Ever Bank Robbery: The Collapse of the Savings and Loan Industry* (New York: Charles Scribner's Sons, 1990).
Mayne, Alan, *Slums: The History of Global Injustice* (London: Reaktion Books, 2017).
McCraw, *The Founders and Finance: How Hamilton, Gallatin, and Others Forged a New Economy* (Cambridge, MA: Belknap/Harvard University Press, 2012).
McDonald, Forrest, "The Intellectual World of the Founding Fathers," National Endowment for the Humanities 1987 Jefferson lecture (Washington, D.C.: Government Printing Office, 1987).
McDonald, Forrest, *We the People: The Economic Origins of the Constitution* (University of Chicago Press, 1958).

Bibliography

McKendrick, Neil, *The Birth of the Consumer Society: The Commercialization of Eighteenth-Century England* (London; Europa Publications, 1982).

Merry, Robert W., *President McKinley: Architect of the American Century* (New York: Simon & Schuster, 2017).

Mills, C. Wright, *White Collar: The American Middle Classes* (New York: Oxford University Press, 1951).

Molotch, Harvey, "The City as a Growth Machine: Toward a Political Economy of Place." *American Journal of Sociology*, vol. 82, no. 2 (Sep. 1976).

Molotch, Harvey, *Managed Integration: Dilemmas of Doing Good in the City* (Berkeley: University of Calif. Press, 1972).

Molotch, Harvey, *Urban Fortunes: The Political Economy of Place* (Berkeley: University of California Press, 1987).

Molotch, Harvey, *Where Stuff Comes From: How Toasters, Toilets, Cars, Computers, and Many Other Things Come to Be as They Are* (New York: Rutledge, 2005).

Monroe, Albert, *How the Federal Housing Administration Affects Homeownership* (Cambridge, MA: Harvard University Department of Economics, 2001)

Moss, Jeremiah, *Vanishing New York: How a Great City Lost Its Soul* (New York: William Morrow, 2017).

Mueller, Jan-Werner, *What Is Populism?* (Philadelphia: University of Pa. Press, 2016).

Mumford, Lewis. *The City in History: Its Origins, Its Transformations, and Its Prospects* (New York, Harcourt, 1961).

Mummery, Albert F., and John A. Hobson, *The Physiology of Industry* (London: John Murray, 1989).

Myrdal, Gunnar, *An American Dilemma: The Negro Problem and American Democracy* (New York: Harper & Brothers, 1944).

Nader Ralph, *Unsafe at Any Speed* (New York: Grossman Publishers, 1965).

Okihiro, Gary Y., *Cane Fires* (Philadelphia: Temple University Press, 1991).

Olney, L. Martha, *Buy Now, Pay Later* (Chapel Hill: University of North Carolina Press,1991).

Packard Vance, *The Hidden Persuaders* (New York: IG Publishers, 1957).

Perlstein, Rick, *Before the Storm: Barry Goldwater and the Unmaking of the American Consensus* (New York: Nation Books, 2009).

Perlstein, Rick, *The Invisible Bridge: The Fall of Nixon and the Rise of Reagan* (New York: Simon & Schuster, 1914).

Perlstein, Rick, *Reaganland: America's Right Turn, 1976–1980* (New York: Simon & Schuster, 2020).

Piketty, Thomas, *Capital in the Twenty-First Century* (Cambridge, MA: Belknap Press of Harvard University Press, 2014).

Plunz, Richard, *A History of Housing in New York City* (New York: Columbia University Press, 1990).

Potter, David M., *People of Plenty: Economic Abundance and the American Character* (University of Chicago Press, 1954).

President's Research Committee on Social Trends *Recent Social Trends in the United States* (New York: McGraw-Hill, 1933).

Pressman, Steven, *The Legacy of John Kenneth Galbraith* (New York: Routledge, 2013).

Radford, Gail, *Modern Housing for America: Policy Struggles in the New Deal Era* (University of Chicago Press, 1996).

Ransby, Barbara, *Ella Baker and the Black Freedom Movement: A Radical Democratic Vision* (Chapel Hill: University of NC Press, 2003).

Reblando, Jason, *New Deal Utopias* (Heidelberg: Kehrer Verlag 2017).

Reisner, Marc, *Cadillac Desert: The American West and Its Disappearing Water* (New York: Penguin, 1987).

Riesman, David, and Nathan Glazer, *The Lonely Crowd* (New Haven: Yale University Press, 1950).

Bibliography

Riis, Jacob, *How the Other Half Lives: Studies Among the Tenements of New York* (New York: Kessinger Publishing, 2004).
Roberge, Roger A., *The Three-Decker: Structural Correlate of Worcester's Industrial Revolution* (Ph.D. dissertation, Clark University, 1965).
Rosenblum, Jonathan D., *Copper Crucible: How the Arizona Miners' Strike of 1983 Recast Labor-Management Relations in America* (Ithaca, NY: ILR Press, 1995).
Rossellini, Roberto, *La prise de Pouvoir par Louis XIV* (Criterion, 1966).
Rothstein, Richard, *The Color of Law: The Forgotten History of How Our Government Segregated America* (New York: Liveright Pub. Co., 2017).
Rove, Karl, *The Triumph of William McKinley: Why the Election of 1896 Still Matters* (New York: Simon & Schuster, 2015).
Rowan, Jamin Creed, *The Sociable City: An American Tradition* (Philadelphia: University of Pennsylvania Press, 2017).
Rubin, Robert, *In an Uncertain World* (New York: Random House, 2003).
Rusk, David, *Inside Game/Outside Game: Winning Strategies for Urban America* (Wash, DC: Brookings Institution Press, 1999).
Satter, Beryl, *Family Properties: Race, Real Estate, and the Exploitation of Black Urban America* (New York: Henry Holt, 2009).
Savage, Sean J., *Roosevelt: The Party Leader, 1932–1945* (Lexington: University Press of Kentucky, 1991).
Schama, Simon, *The Embarrassment of Riches* (New York: Alfred A. Knopf, 1987).
Schlesinger, Arthur M., Jr., *The Coming of the New Deal* (Boston: Houghton Mifflin, 1958).
Schmitt, Mark, "The Legend of the Powell Memo," *The American Prospect*, Aril 25, 2005. https://prospect.org/article/legend-powell-memo/
Schorske, Carl E., *Fin de Siecle Vienna, Politics and Culture* (New York: Alfred A. Knopf, 1979).
Schuler, Joe, *Building a Legacy: The Bill Pulte Story* (Ecelsior, MN: Sang Froid Press, 2006).
Schuman, Tony, "Labor and Housing in New York City, Architect Herman Jessor and the Cooperative Housing Movement," *Internet Document*.
Schwartz, Alex F., *Housing Policy in the United States*, 3rd ed. (New York: Routledge, 2015).
Schwartz, Alex F., *Housing Policy of the United States* (New York: Routledge 2010).
Schwartz, Joel, *The New York Approach: Robert Moses, Urban Liberals, and Redevelopment of the Inner City* (Columbus: Ohio State University Press, 1993).
Siegler, Richard, and Herbert J. Levy, "Brief History of Cooperative Housing," *Cooperative Housing Journal*, Alexandria VA, 1986.
Simon, William E., *A Time for Truth* (New York: McGraw-Hill, 1978).
Simon, William E., with John E. Caher, *A Time for Reflection: An Autobiography* (Chicago: Regnery Publishing, 2004).
Sinclair, Upton, *The Jungle* (New York: Doubleday, Page, & Co., 1906).
Sloan, Alfred P., with John, McDonald, ed., *My Years with General Motors* (Garden City: Doubleday, 1964).
Smith, Gene, *The Shattered Dream: Herbert Hoover and the Great Depression* (New York: Wm. Morrow & Co., 1970).
Smith Susan J.N. Cook and B.A. Searle. "From Canny Consumer to Care-Full Citizen: Towards a Nation of Home Stewardship," Cultures of Consumption Working Paper No.35 at: http://www.consume.bbk.ac.uk/ publications.html. (forthcoming).
Sombart, Werner, *The Jews and Modern Capitalism* (New York: E. P. Dutton, 1915).
Sombart, Werner, *Why Is There in the United States No Socialism?* (New York: Sharpe, 1976).
Sorkin, Michael, *Theme Park: The New American City and the End of Public Space* (New York: Hill and Wang, 1992).

Bibliography

Stein, Judith, *Pivotal Decade: How the United States Traded Factories for Finance in the Seventies* (New Haven: Yale University Press, 2010).
Stein, Judith, *Running Steel, Running America: Race, Economic Policy, and the Decline of America* (Chapel Hill: University of North Carolina Press, 1998).
Stein, Samuel, *Capital City: Gentrification and the Real Estate State* (New York: Verso, 2019).
Stern, Robert M., Thomas Mellins, and Gregory Gilmartin, *New York, 1930: Architecture and*
Strauss, Samuel, "Things Are in the Saddle," *The Atlantic Monthly*, Nov. 1924.
Sugrue, Thomas J., *The Origins of the Urban Crisis* (Princeton, NJ: Princeton University Press, 1996).
Szatmary, David P., *Shay's Rebellion: The Making of An Agrarian Insurrection* (Amherst: University of Massachusetts Press, 1980).
Taibbi, Matt, *The Divide: American Injustice in the Age of the Wealth Gap* (New York: Spiegel & Grau, 2014).
Tarullo, Daniel K., "Financial Stability Regulation," (Philadelphia, PA: Lecture, University of Pa. Law School, Oct. 10, 2012).
Taylor, Keeanga-Yamahtta, "How Real Estate Segregated America," *Dissent*, Fall, 2018.
Temin, Peter, *The Vanishing Middle Class* (Cambridge, MA: MIT Press, 2017).
Tooze, Adam, *Crashed: How a Decade of Financial Crises Changes the World* (New York: Viking, 2018).
Traub, James, *What Was Liberalism? The Past, Present, and Promise of a Noble Idea* (New York Basic Books, 2019).
Treat, Payson Jackson, *The National Land System* (Buffalo, NY: Wm. S. Hein & Co., 2003).
Trentmann, Frank, *Empire of Things: How We Became a World of Consumers, from the Fifteenth Century to the Twenty-First* (New York: Harper, 2017).
Trentmann, Frank, ed. *The Making of the Consumer: Knowledge, Power and Identity in the Modern World* (Oxford and New York: Berg, 2006).
Vale, Lawrence J., *Reclaiming Public Housing: A Half Century of Struggle in Three Public Neighborhoods* (Cambridge, MA: Harvard University Press, 2002).
Wagner-Rieger, Renate, *The Ringstrasse: Image of an Era: The Expansion of the Inner City of Vienna under Emperor Franz Joseph* (Vienna: University of Vienna Press, 1969).
Waldie, D. J., *Holy Land: A Suburban Memoir* (New York: Norton, 1996).
Waldman, Louis, *Labor Lawyer* (New York: E.P. Dutton & Co., 1944).
Waller, Willard, *The Veteran Comes Back* (NY: Dryden Press, 1944).
Wapshott, Nicholas, *Keynes Hayek: The Clash that Defined Modern Economics* (New York: Norton, 2011).
Warner, Sam Bass, Jr., *Streetcar Suburbs: The Process of Growth in Boston, 1870–1900*, 2nd ed. (Cambridge, MA: Harvard University Press, 1962).
Wasserman, Janek, *The Marginal Revolutionaries: How Austrian Economists Fought the War of Ideas* (New Haven: Yale University Press, 2020).
Webb, Sidney and B Webb, *Industrial Democracy* (London: Longmans, Green, 1897).
White, Lawrence J., *The S&L Debacle: Public Policy Lessons for Bank and Thrift Regulation* (New York: Oxford University Press, 1991).
Wilkerson, Isabel, *The Warmth of Other Suns: The Epic Story of America's Great Migration* (New York: Vintage, 2010).
Williams, Charles, "The Racial Politics of Progressive Americanism: New Deal Liberalism and the Subordination of Black Workers in the UAW," *Studies in American Political Development*, 2005, 19 (1).
Wilmarth, Arthur, "Does Financial Liberalization Increase the Likelihood of a Systemic Banking Crisis? Evidence from the Past Three Decades and the Great Depression," in *Too Big to Fail: Policies and Practices in Government Bailouts*, 77–105, edited

Bibliography

by Benton E. Gup. (Westport, CT: Praeger, 2004). (available at http://ssrn.com/abstract=547383).

Wilmarth, Arthur, "How Should We Respond to the Growing Risks of Financial Conglomerates?" in *Banking Law: Financial Modernization after Gramm-Leach-Bliley*, 65–133, edited by Patricia A. McCoy (Newark, NJ: LexisNexis, 2002). (available at http://ssrn.com/abstract=291859).

Wilmarth, Arthur, "The OCC's Preemption Rules Exceed the Agency's Authority and Present a Serious Threat to the Dual Banking System and Consumer Protection." 23 *Annual Review of Banking and Financial Law* 225–364 (2004). Available at http://ssrn.com/abstract=577863.

Wilmarth, Arthur, "The Transformation of the U.S. Financial Services Industry, 1975–2000: Competition, Consolidation, and Increased Risks," 2002 *University of Illinois Law Review*, 215–476 (2002). Available at http://ssrn.com/abstract=315345.

Wood, Edith Elmer, *Recent Trends in American Housing* (New York: Macmillan, 1931).

Woodward, C. Vann, *The Strange Career of Jim Crow* (New York: Oxford University Press, 1955).

Zelizer, Julian, *Burning Down the House: Newt Gingrich, the Fall of a Speaker, and the Rise of a New Republican Party* (New York: Penguin, 2020).

Zipp, Samuel, *Manhattan Projects: The Rise and Fall of Urban Renewal in Cold War New York* (New York: Oxford University Press, 2010).

Zolberg, Aristide, *A Nation by Design: Immigration Policy in the Fashioning of America* (Cambridge, MA: Harvard University Press, 2006).

Index

Adams, James Truslow 47
AFL (American Federation of Labor) 14, 15, 35, 49, 99
Alinsky, Saul 113
Amalgamated Housing Cooperative 44, 53
American Insurance Group (AIG) 141
American Labor Party 16
American Legion 69
Americans for Democratic Action 105
Arsenal of Democracy 64, 65
Arts and Crafts Movement 7
Atlanta Compromise 12, 76, 77

Bank of the United States (BUS) 25
Bankers Trust 22, 26
Banking Act, 1933 (Glass-Steagall) 4, 15, 27, 32
Barkley, Alben 37, 38
Bauer, Catherine 54
Beard, Charles 116
Becontree 69, 70
Berle, Adolf 14, 15, 18, 41, 126
Bernstein, Eduard 107
Bismarck 106
Bonus Army 71
Born, Brooksley 143–151
Boyar, Louis 91
Brabner-Smith, J.W. 61
Brandeis, Louis 15, 18, 21, 26, 41
Buchanan v. Warley 78, 79, 80
Byrnes, James (Jimmy) 87

Capra, Frank 5, 136
Carter, Jimmy 116
Chaplin, Charlie 50
Chicago Freedom Movement 113
Chicopee, MA 91
Cincotta, Gail 113, 114
CIO (Congress of Industrial Organizations) 15, 35, 100, 102

Citigroup 135
Colmery, Harry W. 72
Columbia University 22
Commodity Futures Modernization Act, 2000 143–151
Commodity Futures Trading Commission (CFTC) 143–151
Commonwealth Club Address 18, 27, 44
Community Reinvestment Act, 1977 5, 6, 113, 114, 115, 116
Converse, Edmund C. 26
Council Housing 58, 69
Countrywide Financial (Angelo Mozilo) 139

Daley, Richard 113, 116
Debs, Eugene 17
Democratic Leadership Council 122, 123
Democratic Party, history of 115, 117–124
Depository Institutions Act, 1982 (Garn-St. Germain) 6, 131, 132
Depository Institutions Deregulation & MCA Act, 1980 6, 128, 129
Dochow, Darrel W. 141–142
Dodd, Chris 152–160
Downton Abbey 21
Du Bois W.E.B. 77

Ebbets Field 90
Edina, MN 92
Eisenhower, Dwight D. 117
Ellender, Alan 83
Empire Savings & Loan 129–130
Equal Credit Opportunity Act, 1974 114
Equal Rights Amendment 118

Fair Housing Act, 1968 6, 111
Fannie Mae 4, 60–66
Federal Housing Act, 1934 34, 50, 63, 70, 79, 105, 116, 163

Index

Federal Housing Act, 1937 (Wagner Steagall) 4, 54, 57, 58
Federal Housing Act, 1938 (Steagall-Wagner) 4, 60
Federal Housing Act, 1949 56, 84, 85
Federal National Mortgage Association 60, 61
Federal Reserve Act 18, 20
Financial Institutions Act, 1989 (FIRREA) 6
Financial Services Modernization Act 1999 6, 135
First Homes 52, 56
Ford, Gerald 120, 121
Ford, Henry 36, 47, 49, 99, 126
Ford Motor Company 44, 47, 100
Frank, Barney 152–160
Friedan, Betty 121
Friedman, Milton 40
From, Al 122, 123

Galbraith, John K. 26
General Motors 15, 44; "Sit-Down" Strike, 1937 102
Gibson Greeting Cards 126
Gladwell, Malcolm 94
Glass, Carter 18, 19, 22
Goldman, Marcus 25
Gramschi, Antonio 44
Great Migration 111
Greenspan, Alan 144
Griffith, D.W. 78
Gruen, Victor 92, 93, 94
Gungdong Province 7

Hamilton, Alexander 24, 43
Hanna, Mark 14
Haring, Warren 69, 70
Harlan, John M. 76
Harlem River Houses 55
Hayes, Rutherford B. 11
health coverage 106
Heritage Foundation 121
Hillman, Sidney 45, 53
historically black colleges and universities 73
Hitler, Adolf 64, 88, 102
Home Mortgage Disclosure Act, 1975 114
Home Owners Loan Act, 1933 4, 29, 48, 70
Home Owners Loan Corporation (HOLC) 33, 34, 35, 48
Hoover, Herbert 71

Hoovervilles 71
Housers 54
Humphrey, Hubert H. 82

Ickes, Harold 52

Jackson, Andrew 25
Jackson, Jesse 116, 119
Jefferson, Thomas 24

Karl-Marx-Hof 57
Keynes, John Maynard 2, 27, 37, 38, 41
Knickerbocker Bank 21
Ku Klux Klan 12
Kuhn Loeb 25

Labor-Management Relations Act, 1947 (Taft-Hartley) 16
LaGuardia, Fiorello 53, 54
Lakewood, CA 91
Lawn, IL 111
Lehman Brothers 25
Lenin, V.I. 45
Levitt, Bill 4, 50, 68, 88
Levittown 4, 65, 68, 69
Lewis, John L. 44
Lincoln Savings Bank (Charles Keating) 132–134

Madison, James 24, 25
Marshall, Alfred 3
Marshall, Thurgood 109
Marx, Karl 7, 35
McGovern, George S., 117, 121
McKinley, William 14
McLaurin v. Okla. St. Regents 109
Mellon, Andrew 14
Menger, Carl 162
Moreau, Emile 23
Morgan, J.P. 20, 22, 25
Morgan, Junius 20
Morris, William 7
Mortgage Backed Securities 62
Moses, Robert 53, 83, 84, 85, 87
"Motown" 81
Myrdal, Gunnar 109

NAACP 77
Nader, Ralph 120, 121
National Industrial Recovery Act (NIRA) 15, 54, 56
National Labor Relations Act, 1935 (Wagner Act) 15
New Deal 4, 13, 42, 46, 62, 64

184

Index

Nixon, Richard 121
Norman, Montagu 2
NYCHA (New York City Housing Authority) 52, 53, 55, 86

O'Malley, Walter 90

Palmer, A. Mitchell 101
Plessy v. Ferguson 56, 76
Powell Memo 120
Public Works Administration 52

Quarantine-the-Aggressor 63
Queens (NY borough) 68
Queensbridge Houses 55

Rankin, John E. 72
Reagan, Ronald 120, 122
Red Hook Houses 55
Red-Lining 79, 80
Republican Party, history 13–17
Reuther, Walter 7, 13, 101, 103, 105, 118
Riefler, Winfield 2, 37, 38, 39, 40, 41, 42, 50, 62
Robinson, Jackie 13, 82
Robinson, Sen. Joe 29, 31, 32
Rogers, Edith Nourse 72
Romney, Mitt (Bain Capital) 127
Roosevelt, Franklin D. 12, 44, 49, 71, 80, 116, 159
Roosevelt, Theodore 22, 25
Rove, Karl 14
Rubin, Robert 137, 146–148

Sachs, Samuel 25
Sanders, Bernie 119
Satter, Beryl 111
Schacht, Hjalmar 23
Schelley v. Kraemer 68
Schiff, Jakob 26
Schwartz, Anna J. 40
Sedition Act of 1918 17, 101
Seligman, Edwin R.A. 22
Servicemen's Readjustment Act, 1944 (GI Bill) 4, 67, 105
Servicemen's Readjustment Act, 1945 (amended) 67, 71, 73

Simon, William E. 125
Smith, Al 11, 45
Sombart, Werner 6, 100
Steagall, Rep. Henry 19, 23, 32, 57
Stein, Judith 116
Strong, Benjamin 22, 23, 26
Stuyvesant Town 53, 68, 84
Subprime Mortgage Crisis 6
Suffolk Bank 25
"Sundown" regulations 78
Sweatt v. Painter 109

Taft, Robert 83, 84, 85
Taft-Hartley Labor Relations Act 16
Taper, Mark 91
Technical Bulletin No. 4 46, 50, 58, 66
Techwood Homes 52, 56
TenEyck Houses 55
Thurmond, Strom 13, 82, 105
To Kill a Mockingbird 29, 34
Treaty of Detroit 7, 101, 103, 104
Triborough Bridge 53, 84
Truman, Harry 13, 105
Tudor-Walters Report 57
Tugwell, Rex 45, 46

United Automobile Workers 13, 102, 118
University of Phoenix 140
Unwin, Raymond 57

Veterans of Foreign Wars 69
Vinson, Fred 82

Wagner, Robert 57, 83
Wall Street Reform and Consumer Protection Act, 2010 6, 152–160
Warburg, Paul 22
Washington, Booker T. 12, 76, 77
Watson, Tom 12
Weingart, Ben 91
Wesray Corp. 126
Willingsboro, NJ 113
Wilson, Woodrow 11, 12, 13
Windrip, Berzelius "Buzz" 48
Wood, Grant 65

www.ingramcontent.com/pod-product-compliance
Lightning Source LLC
Chambersburg PA
CBHW032046300426
44117CB00009B/1215